LION HOUSE RECIPES

LION HOUSE RECIPES

Compiled by Helen Thackeray

Photographs by Borge B. Andersen
and Craig W. Dimond

SHADOW MOUNTAIN

Salt Lake City, Utah

*Stuffed pork chop, parslied carrots, baked
potato, Sarah's salad*

Library of Congress Cataloging-in-Publication Data

Main entry under title:

Lion House recipes.

Includes index.
1. Cookery.   I. Thackeray, Helen, 1912–
TX715.L7596   641.5   80-19719
ISBN 0-87747-831-7

Printed in the United States of America

10   9   8   7

Contents

The Lion House   1

Appetizers and Beverages   7

Soups   11

Meats   19

Poultry   37

Fish and Shellfish   46

Vegetables   51

Salads and Salad Dressings   60

Breads and Rolls   75

Cakes, Cake Desserts, and Cookies   82

Pies and Pastries   96

Desserts and Dessert Sauces   107

Index   117

The Lion House

One of Salt Lake City's most famous landmarks is the Lion House, which stands on busy South Temple Street next door to the administration building of The Church of Jesus Christ of Latter-day Saints.

This fine pioneer home was built in 1855-56 by Brigham Young, the great Mormon colonizer, territorial governor, and second president of the Church. Built in the style of early English homes, the Lion House reflects the New England background of Brigham Young. It was designed by Truman O. Angell, architect of the famous Mormon temple on nearby Temple Square in downtown Salt Lake City.

The house gets its name from a stone statue of a reclining lion above the front entrance, the work of William Ward, skilled English craftsman. A decorative iron fence surrounds the front yard, which blooms with colorful flowers from spring through fall. Originally built of adobe and sandstone (which the pioneers called "grindstone" and which was found in nearby canyons), the Lion House today closely resembles the original, which one of Brigham Young's daughters described in her writings as "cream plaster which with white woodwork and green shutters made a very lovely appearance."

One significant event that took place in the Lion House in pioneer times was the organization of an association for young women. On November 28, 1869, after evening prayer in the front parlor, President Young asked his daughters to remain in the parlor. He told them, "I have long had it in my mind to organize the young ladies into an association so that they might assist the older citizens of the valley, the fathers and mothers, in propagating, teaching, and practicing the principles I have been so long teaching." He urged the girls to return to modest standards in their mode of dress and their way of life, rather than follow "the frivolous ways of the world." The organization that he then established is still in existence today, with more than 200,000 young women ages twelve to eighteen actively participating worldwide.

Following Brigham Young's death in 1877, the Lion House remained in the hands of family members for a short time before it was purchased by the Church. It served as office space for a few years, then became a home economics center for the Latter-day Saint University, which was located nearby. When the university closed in 1931, the house was turned over to the young women's organization, to be used as a social center for women and girls. Many cultural events were held there, including receptions, parties, lectures, book reviews, and musical programs.

In 1963 the house was closed for extensive remodeling and modernization, including installation of an elevator and of air conditioning, construction of an additional stairway, expansion of kitchen facilities, and reinforcement with steel beams to make it structurally sound. It was reopened in the fall of 1968 to serve the community as a social center, a place to reflect on the culture and heritage of the pioneers who had settled in the Salt Lake Valley.

As one steps through the imposing front door, he enters the vestibule of the second or main floor, where the parlor and several sitting rooms were located in pioneer times. The parlor was an elegant room, with a "store-boughten" carpet, imported Nottingham curtains, velvet draperies, and fine Victorian furniture. Here the family gathered for daily prayer and for counsel from the head of the family. Today the parlor has many furnishings and artifacts from Brigham Young's day, including the bell he used to summon his family to prayer.

Also on this floor are four other rooms that today are used for small luncheons, dinner parties, and receptions: the 1875 Room, the Social Room, the Pioneer Room, and the Garden Room. The latter opens out onto a beautiful backyard garden, where an old water pump stands over the original well.

A children's party room is to the right of the vestibule. A warm, cheerful room dominated by a fireplace with a reclining lion statue beside it, this is the setting for children's parties six days a week. Here children can come on their birthdays and other special occasions to learn of their pioneer heritage. Hostesses teach them pioneer games and tell them stories of pioneer times.

The third floor of the Lion House originally had twenty bedrooms, ten on each side of the long central hall, with a small fireplace and a dormer window in each room. The walls separating the bedrooms have been removed, and three large reception rooms are now located there, with sliding partitions dividing them.

The largest of the rooms is the Banquet Room, which can seat up to one hundred people. Next to this is the Gable Room, and then the Buffet Room. When all three rooms are opened up, groups of as many as two hundred can be accommodated. A modern kitchen, pantries, and storage rooms are also on this floor, to service the many wedding receptions, dinners, and other parties held there almost every week night of the year.

Both the second and the third floors have beautiful hardwood floors and furniture. Realizing that hardwood would be scarce in the Rocky Mountains, President Young instructed the pioneers to build their wagons and packing boxes of hardwood for future use, and to pack panes of glass between layers of bedding; some of this glass was used in the Lion House.

The finest furnishings have been used throughout the home. Ingrained carpets woven to a design of the pioneer period cover the second and third floors. Damask, brocade, mohair, dimity, and other luxurious fabrics of pioneer times have been used in upholstery and window coverings. Some of the furniture was originally in the home; other pieces have been located in homes, garages, antique shops, and stores throughout the country. Among the beautiful antiques are two crystal chandeliers that were once used in the New Hampshire governor's mansion.

The hub of family activity in the Lion House in Brigham Young's day was the first (street-level) floor, which featured a long dining room where as many as seventy family members and guests ate. Other rooms on this floor included large vegetable and fruit cellars; a weaving room where carpets and cloth were woven; a milk room for storage of milk, cream, butter, and cheese; a laundry room; pantries and cupboards; bathrooms; and a huge kitchen. In one corner was a room that served as a schoolroom until a schoolhouse could be completed; then the room became the family's recreation room. Here the children gathered for parties and entertainments. Large steel hooks were attached to the walls for pulling taffy or vinegar candy, and there was a small stove for popping corn.

Today the first floor of the Lion House is home to the Lion House Pantry, a cafeteria where the famous Lion House food is served to people who buy membership cards that entitle them and their guests to eat lunch there Mondays through Fridays. Hostesses greet the members and guests in the Welcome Room, which is furnished with antique kitchen utensils, a big butcher block table featuring a centerpiece of fresh vegetables and fruits, and an inviting fireplace. After going through the cafeteria line and selecting from the many entrées, soups, salads, breads, and desserts prepared each day, patrons may then eat in any of the four dining rooms or, if the weather is warm, in the garden outside. Diners exit through the Welcome Room, where the hostesses have items available for purchase to take back to the office or home: whole wheat bread, date-nut bread, horehound and peppermint candies, shiny red apples, and honey butter. Pies, cakes, rolls, cookies, and other treats may be ordered in advance and picked up there.

The Lion House has a well-deserved reputation for excellent food at reasonable prices. The party rooms on the second and third floors are often booked for months or even years in advance for wedding breakfasts and receptions, luncheons, dinner parties, family reunions, and other party occasions.

Often, when family members plan a golden wedding celebration for a couple, they discover that the couple's wedding reception had also been held at the Lion House fifty years before. And the second and even third generations of many families hold their wedding receptions where once their parents and grandparents had greeted their own wedding guests.

For their wedding breakfast or luncheon, a bridal couple might choose the house specialty: French onion soup gratinée, tossed green salad, chicken Cordon Bleu, Oriental vegetables, hot fresh rolls, and mint parfait. Or they may prefer the hunter's breakfast special: chilled fruit juice, melon with strawberries, scrambled eggs with fresh sliced mushrooms, ham, blueberry muffins, and potatoes lyonnaise. The wedding party menu also offers numerous other appetizers, salads, entrées, and desserts for those who wish to make up their own menu.

Wedding receptions might feature petits fours, eclairs, cream puffs, fruit platters, nut breads, carrot cake, strawberry tarts, open-face sandwiches, frappé—or such unusual items as cold cucumber soup, quiche lorraine, clam chowder, or, in winter, hot wassail.

The luncheon and banquet menus have large selections of appetizers (spiced apple juice, fresh fruit cup, Canadian cheese soup, spiced tomato soup, cream of fresh mushroom soup, for example), salads (such as pear blush, fruit and cream, Waldorf, and Caesar salads), entrées (prime rib of beef, tournedos Rossini, baked salmon steak, Australian lobster tail, chicken Alabam, stuffed pork chops), with choice of vegetables, potatoes, and desserts (pies and tarts, cakes, parfaits, and cheesecake).

Where do Lion House recipes come from? Over the years dozens of good cooks have been employed to turn out the oh-so-good food enjoyed in the cafeteria and the party rooms, men and women who love to cook and who have reputations for excellence in their culinary efforts. Each one has brought favorite recipes used to express love for loved ones. It is from these recipes that selections have been made for inclusion in *Lion House Recipes*.

In addition, some of the cooks on the Lion House board of directors were invited to submit some of their own favorite recipes to help add balance to the collection.

Of necessity, recipes that must be cut down from cafeteria or party size to smaller family sizes must be changed somewhat. Also, some steps in preparation are just not practicable for use at home, and occasionally some ingredients are not readily available to the home cook. Each recipe in this book has been tested carefully to be sure it works for home cooks, and the results are as close as possible to the Lion House dishes.

All of the Lion House recipes are special, representing the tastiest, most appetizing dishes from a home that is well known for its superb cuisine. The staff and management worked on this cookbook for four years to ensure that it would meet their high standards for excellence. Now these exceptional recipes are available here, under one cover, for you and your family to enjoy!

The Lion House Children's Party

An exciting event takes place almost daily in the Children's Room at the Lion House—a party! This is a special occasion for a child to be recognized and honored on his or her birthday, and for all of the guests to learn of their pioneer heritage.

As they arrive, the children are greeted by a hostess, who will teach them pioneer games, tell them stories of pioneer times, and supervise their refreshment time. Each child wears a pioneer hat or Indian headdress during the party and a big "Brigham Young bib" at refreshment time.

The children tour the Lion House and learn that the pioneers worked hard to grow their own vegetables and wheat. They also had to grow their own spices, and a favorite of these spices was ginger, from which gingerbread cookies were made. Each guest is given a gingerbread cookie in the shape of a heart, while the child being honored that day receives a cookie in the shape of a lion.

The children learn that in Brigham Young's day, children were allowed to have friends visit at least once a week to pull taffy, pop corn, or make a freezer of ice cream. President Young tried to make the birthday of each of his fifty-six children a very special day, with the gift of a "pioneer package" containing twelve raisins (representing the twelve months of the year), some sugar cubes (a favorite sweet treat), and sunflower nuts, which grew abundantly in the Salt Lake Valley. The child who is being honored in modern times is given a "pioneer present" as well as a stuffed toy train as a memento of his or her memorable party at the Lion House.

Refreshment time is a highlight of the birthday party, as the children enjoy ribbon sandwiches, celery and carrot sticks, fruit punch, ice cream, and a delicious birthday cake made and decorated by the Lion House cooks.

A most popular activity for the children is to make taffy from an old-fashioned recipe. When the taffy cools enough to be handled, the children pull it and then form their initials, a treat that they can take home. Here is the recipe they follow:

Lion House Taffy

2 cups sugar
1½ cups water
1 cup white corn syrup
1 teaspoon salt
2 teaspoons glycerine*
1 teaspoon vanilla
2 tablespoons butter

Mix sugar, water, corn syrup, salt, and glycerine in a heavy saucepan. Bring to a boil and cook to a temperature of 258 degrees F. Remove from heat and let stand for two to three minutes. Then add vanilla and butter and stir vigorously until butter is melted. Pour into buttered cookie sheet. Cool until lukewarm taffy can be handled comfortably.

Wash and dry your hands thoroughly. Then take a small piece of taffy and stretch and fold, stretch and fold, stretch and fold, until taffy turns white and pliable. Form your initial on a square of wax paper. (Long strips of taffy may also be cut into 1-inch pieces and wrapped in pieces of wax paper or plastic wrap.)

Glycerine can be purchased from a drugstore and is an important ingredient in this recipe.

Appetizers and Beverages

Cheese Appetizers

Mix together ½ cup (¼ pound) butter and 1 cup flour. Blend in ½ pound (about 2 cups) grated sharp cheese. Roll into small balls, then flatten with a fork and place on an ungreased baking sheet. Bake at 375 degrees F. for 8 to 10 minutes. Makes about 3 dozen small appetizers.

Cheese Ball

    1 8-ounce package cream cheese
    1 5-ounce jar blue cheese spread
    1 cup shredded sharp Cheddar cheese
    Garlic salt
    Celery salt
    Onion salt
    Chopped parsley or nuts

Beat cheeses together until smooth. Add seasonings to taste. Form into a ball and roll in chopped parsley or nuts. Makes 25 servings.

Open-Face Chicken Sandwiches

    2 cups ground chicken meat (canned chicken may be used)
    1 can (8 ounces) crushed pineapple, drained
    ½ cup slivered almonds, chopped
    Salt to taste
    Lemon juice to taste (about 2 teaspoons)
    Mayonnaise (about 3 tablespoons, to make of spreading consistency)

Combine all ingredients and stir until well blended. Taste to correct seasonings. Cover and refrigerate until ready to use. Spread on slices of bread cut into fancy shapes.

Party Roll-Ups

    12 thin slices white bread
    8 slices bacon, cooked, drained, and crumbled
    2 packages (3 ounces each) cream cheese, softened
    12 spears asparagus, cooked and cooled
    Melted butter

Trim crusts from slices of bread; roll with rolling pin to flatten slightly. Blend bacon bits with cream cheese and spread mixture on bread slices. Lay one cooled asparagus spear on each slice of bread and roll up. Place on baking sheet, seam side down. Cover and refrigerate until serving time.

Brush with melted butter and toast at 350 degrees F. until lightly browned, about 15 to 18 minutes. Serve hot. Makes 12 appetizers.

Ribbon Sandwiches

    1 unsliced sandwich loaf, chilled
    Butter or margarine, softened
    1 cup each of 3 different fillings (below)
    2 packages (8 ounces each) cream cheese, softened
    ⅓ cup milk
    Snipped parsley

Slice bread lengthwise in 4 layers; trim crusts. Butter layers. Spread first layer with one of the fillings; arrange on serving tray. Spread another filling on second layer and place over first layer, using 2 spatulas to support layers. Spread another filling on third layer. Fit into position on second layer. Wrap in foil; chill.

At serving time, beat cream cheese with milk until fluffy. Frost top and sides of loaf. Sprinkle frosted loaf with snipped parsley. Makes 10 slices.

Note: You may frost the loaf early; cover loosely and chill until serving time.

Cheese Filling

1 jar (5 ounces) American cheese
1 package (3 ounces) cream cheese
1 tablespoon mayonnaise (more or less as needed)
¼ cup minced pimiento

Combine ingredients together. Beat until smooth.

Ham Filling

1 cup finely chopped fully cooked ham
¼ cup mayonnaise
2 tablespoons dill pickle relish, drained
1 teaspoon prepared horseradish
1 teaspoon prepared mustard
1 tablespoon chopped green onion

Combine ingredients and mix thoroughly.

Egg Salad Filling

4 hard-cooked eggs, chopped fine
⅓ cup chopped ripe olives
2 tablespoons chopped green onions or chives
2 teaspoons prepared mustard
¼ cup mayonnaise (more or less, as needed)
½ teaspoon salt

Combine ingredients. Taste to correct seasoning.

Cream Cheese Filling

1 package (8 ounces) cream cheese, softened
¼ cup nuts, chopped
1 small can (2¼ ounces) chopped ripe olives
2 tablespoons mayonnaise (more or less, as needed)

Combine ingredients and mix thoroughly.

Guacamole

1 large ripe avocado
1 teaspoon finely chopped green onion
¼ teaspoon salt
Dash of oregano
2 teaspoons lemon juice
Few drops Tabasco sauce (optional)
Chopped jalapeno peppers (optional)

Peel avocado and remove stone. Place in small bowl and mash with fork. Add green onion, salt, and oregano. Mash together thoroughly. Add lemon juice and mix again. If you want guacamole to be hot, add Tabasco sauce and chopped jalapeno peppers, according to taste. Makes about ⅔ cup.

Spinach Dip

1 package (10 ounces) frozen spinach
½ pint sour cream (about)
¾ teaspoon salt
⅛ teaspoon white pepper
⅛ teaspoon onion juice or finely chopped onion
⅛ teaspoon Worcestershire sauce
4 drops hot sauce
⅛ teaspoon monosodium glutamate

Cook spinach according to package directions. Drain, then place in strainer or colander and run cold water over it. This keeps the color green. Squeeze or mash so that all water is removed and spinach is very dry. Put spinach in blender and chop well. Add enough sour cream to moisten to dip consistency, then add remaining ingredients and blend just until combined. Correct seasonings. Chill before serving.

Hot Zippity Tomato Dill Drink

1 can (46 ounces) tomato juice
4 tablespoons sugar
1 teaspoon salt
¼ teaspoon garlic salt
2 tablespoons Worcestershire sauce
3 dashes Tabasco sauce
½ cup dill pickle juice
⅓ cup lemon juice

Combine all ingredients in saucepan. Bring mixture to a boil. Let stand awhile to develop flavors. Taste to correct seasonings. Beverage may be served hot or cold. Garnish with chopped chives or a dollop of sour cream, if desired. Makes 7 cups, about 12 servings.

Tomato Tune Up

3 cups tomato juice
½ cup sliced celery
2 thin slices onion
1 bay leaf
4 whole cloves
2 dashes Tabasco sauce
1 cup beef broth
4 thin slices lemon, halved

In saucepan combine tomato juice, celery, onion, bay leaf, and cloves. Bring to a boil and add Tabasco sauce. Reduce heat and cover. Let simmer for 20 minutes. Strain soup, discarding seasonings. Return to saucepan and add broth. Bring to a second boil. Serve in soup bowls; float halved lemon slice in each bowl. Makes 4 servings, 1 cup each.

Hot Tomato Drink

1 large can (46 ounces) tomato juice
1 large can (46 ounces) vegetable juice cocktail
2 cans (10½ ounces) consommé, undiluted
1 can (10½ ounces) tomato soup
1 soup can water
Seasoned salt, celery salt, and onion salt
1 cup heavy cream, whipped

Heat juices, consommé, soup, water, and seasonings to boiling. Strain and cool. When ready to serve, top with whipped cream. Serve either hot or cold. Makes about 4 quarts.

Ice Cream Apricot Nectar

1 cup chilled apricot nectar
2 teaspoons lemon juice
Pinch of salt
1 tablespoon sugar
1 large scoop vanilla ice cream

Put apricot nectar into blender. Add lemon juice, salt, and sugar. Add ice cream and blend until ice cream half melts. Serve at once. Makes 2 cups.

Tangy Shrimp Appetizer

3 cans broken shrimp
1 envelope dry onion soup mix
2 cans (46 ounces each) vegetable juice cocktail
2 cans (15 ounces each) chicken broth
¼ cup lemon juice
3 cups finely diced celery
¼ cup sugar
Salt and pepper to taste

Rinse shrimp in cold water and drain. Combine with remaining ingredients. Refrigerate overnight to blend flavors. When ready to serve, heat in a large saucepan. Pour into punch cups for appetizer or into soup bowls for soup course. Makes 30 punch cups or 15 1-cup servings.

Banana Freeze

4 cups sugar
6 cups water
5 oranges
2 lemons
5 bananas
1 quart apricot or pineapple juice

Boil the sugar and water three to five minutes, until sugar is well dissolved; cool. Squeeze the juice from the oranges and lemons. Mash the bananas. Combine the orange and lemon juices, mashed bananas, and apricot or pineapple juice. Add to sugar and water mixture and freeze. When ready to serve, chop and spoon into sherbet dishes or punch cups and pour lemon-lime carbonated beverage over it.

Grenadine Freeze

1 cup sugar
2 cups water
2 cups grapefruit juice
½ cup grenadine syrup
1 tablespoon lemon juice
1 16-ounce bottle lemon-lime carbonated beverage
1 thinly sliced lemon
Maraschino cherries

Boil sugar and water together. Stir until sugar is dissolved. Remove from heat. Add grapefruit juice, grenadine syrup, and lemon juice. Freeze. To serve, chop frozen mixture and place into serving cups. Pour lemon-lime drink over top and garnish with lemon slice and maraschino cherry half. Makes 14 one-half-cup servings.

Fruit Freeze

2 cans (about 16 ounces each) grapefruit
    segments, undrained
1 can (11 ounces) Mandarin oranges, undrained
½ cup sugar
1 small jar maraschino cherries, undrained
1 can (about 20 ounces) crushed pineapple,
    undrained
1 bottle (12 ounces) lemon-lime carbonated
    beverage
1 pint lime sherbet

Whirl grapefruit sections, oranges, and sugar together in blender for about 30 seconds. Chop cherries; add cherries, cherry juice, and crushed pineapple to blended fruits. Pour into freezer trays or loaf pans and freeze. When ready to serve, chop frozen mixture and spoon into serving cups. Pour on lemon-lime drink and top with a small scoop of sherbet. Makes 15 to 20 punch cup servings.

Three-Fruit Slush

1 cup sugar
2 cups water
2 cups mashed bananas (4 to 6)
½ cup fresh lemon juice
1 6-ounce can frozen lemonade, no water added
1 6-ounce can frozen orange juice, 3 cans water
    added

Combine sugar and water, and boil together about 3 minutes. Cool. Mash bananas; add to fruit juices and sugar syrup. Pour into pans for freezing; freeze until slushy. Stir occa-sionally. Remove from pan to beat with an egg beater once during freezing, if desired. Makes about 20 appetizer servings. Serve it plain or pour ginger ale or similar carbonated beverage over it just before serving.

Wassail

½ cup sugar
2 cups water
5 whole cloves
4 allspice berries
1 cinnamon stick
½ piece ginger root
2 cups orange juice
1 cup lemon juice
1 quart apple cider or juice

Combine sugar and water; boil 2 minutes. Remove from heat and add spices. Cover and allow to stand in a warm place for 1 hour. Strain. Add juices and cider. Bring quickly to a boil. Remove from heat and serve at once. Makes about 8 cups.

Fruit Punch with Sherbet

2 large cans (46 ounces each) pineapple-
    grapefruit juice
1 can (6 ounces) frozen lemon juice
1 can (6 ounces) frozen lime juice
2 cans water
2 shakes salt
1 quart lime sherbet
2 quarts ginger ale

Mix fruit juices, water, and salt, and let stand overnight in refrigerator. Before serving, add lime sherbet and ginger ale. Makes 30 punch cup servings.

Soups

Brown Soup Stock

1 or 2 marrow bones, cracked
4 pounds beef shin, cut in small pieces
3 quarts cold water
⅓ cup each chopped celery, carrots, onion, white turnips
2 sprigs parsley, chopped
5 whole cloves
8-10 peppercorns
1 bay leaf
¼ teaspoon each marjoram and thyme
1 tablespoon salt

Scrape marrow from bones; melt in kettle over moderate heat. Brown about half of beef in marrow fat. Add remaining beef shin, bones, and water; cover and bring to boil slowly. Remove scum. Add vegetables and seasonings; cover and simmer gently about 4 hours, removing scum occasionally. Strain, chill, remove fat, and strain again. Use for soups and sauces. Makes about 2 quarts stock.

Note: Vegetables and seasonings may be varied as desired. For added flavor, vegetables may be simmered in butter for 10 minutes before adding to soup.

Chicken Stock

4 pounds chicken, quartered or cut in pieces
Chicken giblets (optional)
1 teaspoon salt
4 ribs celery, cut in 3-inch pieces
3 carrots, cut in 3-inch pieces
1 medium onion, cloves stuffed in each end of onion
1 large leek, sliced (optional)
¼ cup fresh chopped parsley

Place chicken and giblets in large saucepan. Cover with cold water; add salt. Bring to a boil slowly and simmer until chicken is almost tender. Remove scum from surface as it forms. Add celery, carrot, onion, and leek. Simmer until chicken is fork tender. Remove from heat. Add parsley and let stand 30 minutes.

Remove chicken; strain stock through cheesecloth that has been placed in strainer. Skim fat off as it comes to top. (This is easier to do if the stock is chilled, or with a fat-skimming whisk.) Stock can be frozen and used when needed.

Chicken may be used in a variety of creamed dishes. Remove skin and bones and cut meat in cubes. Meat may also be frozen for later use.

Mongolian Hot Pot

½ pound bacon, diced
1 pound lean ground beef or 2 cups diced cooked ham
1 can (10½ ounces) condensed beef broth or 3 teaspoons beef soup base
1 quart water
1 onion, chopped
1 green pepper, chopped
1 carrot, sliced
1 tablespoon soy sauce
1 can (16 ounces) tomatoes
1 package (10 ounces) frozen mixed vegetables
1 zucchini, sliced
2 teaspoons salt
⅛ teaspoon pepper
1 tablespoon finely chopped parsley (optional)

Fry bacon in large, heavy saucepan until crisp; drain on absorbent paper. Pour off all but 2 tablespoons bacon fat. Sauté beef or ham in the 2 tablespoons bacon fat. Add next seven ingredients and simmer gently for about 1 hour. Add mixed vegetables and zucchini, and simmer another 10 minutes. Add salt and pepper. Taste to correct seasoning. Add chopped parsley just before serving. Makes about 10 cups, or 10 one-cup servings.

Roux

The Lion House uses roux to thicken soups. The amount used depends upon individual taste.

Mix 2 cups flour and 1 cup butter or margarine together until well blended. Store in refrigerator. When ready to use, add to hot liquid a little at a time. Stir constantly until the preferred consistency is reached.

Chilled Cucumber Soup

    2 onions, chopped
    2 cucumbers, peeled and chopped
    2 leeks (white part), chopped (or green onions
        may be used)
    ¼ pound butter or margarine
    2 cups chicken stock
    Salt (½ to 1 teaspoon)
    ⅛ teaspoon white pepper
    1 tablespoon butter or margarine
    1 tablespoon flour
    ½ cup heavy cream
    1 teaspoon dill weed
    ½ teaspoon lemon juice
    Few drops hot pepper sauce
    1 cucumber, peeled, seeded, and chopped

Cook onions, 2 cucumbers, and leek in butter until soft but not brown. Add stock, salt, and pepper and bring to a boil. Whisk in the 1 tablespoon butter and flour made into a roux. Simmer gently for 30 minutes to develop the flavor.

Remove from heat and whirl in a blender until smooth. Strain purée into a bowl and add cream, dill weed, lemon juice, hot pepper sauce, and chopped cucumber. Chill thoroughly. Taste to correct seasonings and serve. Makes about 6 servings.

Vegetable Soup

    1 cup diced tomatoes
    1½ cups diced carrots
    1 cup diced celery
    1½ quarts water
    ¼ cup chopped onion
    1 tablespoon beef soup base
    ½ cup green beans
    1 cup diced potatoes
    ½ pound cooked beef pieces
    1 cup peas

Cook together tomatoes, carrots, celery, water, onion, and beef soup base until carrots and celery are tender. Add beans, potatoes, and beef and an additional cup of water. Simmer until vegetables are tender. Add peas about 5 minutes before serving. Taste to correct seasoning. Makes 3 quarts, about 12 one-cup servings.

Minestrone

    1 cup navy beans
    ½ pound diced bacon
    ⅓ pound diced ham
    ½ cup chopped onion
    2 cups beef stock
    1½ cups canned tomatoes
    1½ cups chopped carrots
    1 cup green beans
    1 cup chopped cabbage
    1 cup chopped celery
    1 cup spaghetti, broken into pieces
    Few grains salt and pepper

Soak beans overnight in water to cover. Boil beans in soaking water until tender (about 2 hours). Add more water as needed. Cook bacon until crisp; drain, and crumble. Sauté ham and onion in bacon fat. Add to beans the beef stock, bacon, ham, and onion, along with tomatoes, carrots, green beans, cabbage, celery, and spaghetti. Cook until the fresh vegetables are tender (10 to 15 minutes). Taste and add salt and pepper as desired. Makes about 3 quarts (12 one-cup servings).

Carrot Apple Bisque

5 to 6 large carrots, peeled
1 tablespoon butter or margarine
About 4 cups chicken broth
1 large apple or ½ cup unsweetened applesauce
½ cup light cream
½ teaspoon nutmeg
⅓ cup minced green onion, including some of the tops

Cut carrots into ½-inch chunks. Combine in a saucepan with butter and 1 cup of the chicken broth. Cook, covered, until carrots are very tender, about 20 minutes. Meanwhile peel, core, and slice apple, adding it (or applesauce) to carrots for the last 5 minutes. Remove pan from heat, uncover, and allow to cool for about 10 minutes.

Whirl carrot mixture in a blender until smooth, or force mixture through a strainer. Stir in the light cream and nutmeg; stir in remaining chicken broth until soup is desired consistency. Serve hot, or cover and refrigerate to serve cold. Sprinkle with chopped green onion. Makes 6 to 8 servings.

Cucumber Soup

½ onion, chopped
2 tablespoons butter
1½ pounds cucumbers (about 8), peeled and chopped
1½ teaspoons white wine vinegar
¾ teaspoon dried dill weed or tarragon leaves
6 cups chicken stock
4 tablespoons cream of wheat (quick-cooking cereal), or use roux to make desired consistency
1 cup sour cream
Salt and pepper
¼ cup chopped parsley

Sauté onion in butter in a heavy pan until transparent. Add cucumbers, vinegar, dill weed, and chicken stock. Bring to a boil; simmer until cucumbers are tender.

Thicken with cream of wheat. Add more chicken stock if a thinner consistency is desired. Purée mixture in a blender. Cool. When cool, work in sour cream until consistency you want. Add salt and pepper to taste. Chill. Garnish with a thin slice of cucumber and a small dab of sour cream, and sprinkle with chopped parsley. Makes about 14 cups.

Gazpacho

1 clove garlic
4 ripe tomatoes, peeled and quartered
½ large green pepper, seeded and sliced
½ small onion, peeled and sliced
1 cucumber, peeled and sliced
1 teaspoon salt
¼ teaspoon pepper
2 tablespoons olive oil
3 tablespoons vinegar
½ cup ice water

Fill blender container with vegetables; add seasonings, olive oil, vinegar, and water. (Use about half the ingredients at one time.) Cover and blend for just 2 seconds. Chill in refrigerator or pour into soup plates and serve with an ice cube in the center of each serving. Makes 6 servings.

Chicken and Corn Chowder

¼ cup chopped onion
2 tablespoons chopped green pepper
2 tablespoons butter or margarine
3 cups milk
1 can (10½ ounces) cream of chicken soup
1 can (12 or 16 ounces) corn niblets, undrained
1 teaspoon chicken soup base
¼ teaspoon salt

Cook onions and pepper in butter until soft but not browned. Add remaining ingredients; simmer for about 5 minutes to develop flavor. For a heartier soup, minced chicken may be added as desired. Thicken with a little roux, if desired. Makes 5 to 6 cups, about 6 servings.

Golden Squash Soup

1 small onion, sliced
2 tablespoons butter or margarine
¼ cup flour
5 cups milk
1½ cups winter squash (hubbard, banana, etc.), cooked and puréed
1½ teaspoons salt
¼ teaspoon celery salt
⅛ teaspoon curry powder
Pepper to taste
2 tablespoons parsley, chopped

Cook onion in butter in a large saucepan for a few minutes. Blend flour with onion; add milk. Cook over low heat, stirring constantly, until thickened. Remove from heat; gently blend in squash and seasoning. Heat to serving temperature but do not boil. Sprinkle each serving of soup with parsley.

Note: A 12-ounce package of frozen puréed squash may be used in this recipe. Add squash; continue to heat soup only until squash is defrosted. Makes 6 servings, 1 cup each.

Zucchini Soup

3 cups (about 1 pound) sliced zucchini
½ cup water
1 tablespoon fresh or instant minced onion
1 teaspoon seasoned salt
½ teaspoon parsley flakes (or 2 tablespoons chopped fresh parsley)
2 teaspoons chicken soup base or 2 bouillon cubes
2 tablespoons butter or margarine
2 tablespoons flour
⅛ teaspoon white pepper
⅛ teaspoon monosodium glutamate (MSG)
1 cup milk
½ cup light cream
Paprika
Sour cream

Combine zucchini, water, onion, seasoned salt, parsley, and 1 teaspoon soup base. Cook until zucchini is tender and most of water has

evaporated. Mash or purée and set aside.

In saucepan melt butter; add flour and rest of soup base, pepper, and monosodium glutamate. Blend; add milk and cream and simmer until thickened. Stir in puréed vegetables; thin with milk, if desired. Garnish with paprika and sour cream. Taste to correct seasoning. Makes 4 to 6 servings.

Spiced Tomato Soup

1 can (46 ounces) tomato juice
1 tablespoon sugar
1 tablespoon chicken soup base
3 cups water
2 tablespoons taco seasoning (or to taste)

Combine ingredients and bring to a boil. Taste to correct seasoning. Serve hot or cold. Makes 8 to 10 servings.

Potato and Onion Chowder

1 cup diced onions
½ cup finely chopped celery
2 tablespoons butter or margarine
1 can (about 13 ounces) condensed chicken broth
1 teaspoon salt
Dash of pepper
2 cups cubed or sliced raw potatoes
1½ cups milk
½ cup light cream
1 teaspoon chopped parsley

Sauté onions and celery in butter until transparent, but not browned. Add chicken broth, salt, pepper, and potatoes. Cover and bring to a boil. Reduce heat and boil gently until potatoes are tender, about 20 minutes. Add milk, light cream, and parsley. Heat thoroughly. Makes about 5 servings.

Macaroni and Tomato Soup

2 tablespoons butter or margarine
½ cup onion, chopped
¼ cup diced green pepper
1 cup diced celery
1 can (10½ ounces) tomato soup
1 can water
1 can (46 ounces) tomato juice
4 ounces macaroni, cooked
Dash pepper
½ teaspoon salt (or more to taste)
½ teaspoon sweet basil
1 tablespoon sugar
1 to 2 bay leaves

In heavy saucepan, melt butter; cook onion, green pepper, and celery until limp but not brown. Add remaining ingredients. Heat to boiling. Makes 10 to 12 one-cup servings.

Hearty Chicken Noodle Soup

2 teaspoons chicken soup base
3 cups chicken soup stock
2 cups chopped carrots
2 cups chopped celery
¾ cup chopped onion
2 cans (about 10 ounces) cream of chicken
   soup
¼ cup evaporated milk or ½ cup whole milk
Roux (see page 12)
2 cups cooked diced chicken
2½ ounces (about 4 cups) cooked noodles
Salt and pepper to taste

Heat chicken soup base and stock together. Add carrots, celery, and onions, and simmer until vegetables are tender. Add cream of chicken soup and milk. Thicken with roux as desired, then add cooked chicken and noodles. Add salt and pepper, and taste to correct seasonings. Makes about 2½ quarts, or 10 one-cup servings.

Western Tomato Soup

3 slices bacon, cooked and crumbled
½ cup finely chopped celery
3 tablespoons finely chopped onions
¼ cup finely chopped green peppers
3 tablespoons flour
2 cups milk
1 can (10½ ounces) tomato soup
2 cups (or 1 16-ounce can) stewed tomatoes
1½ cups tomato juice
Salt and pepper to taste

Sauté celery, onion, and green pepper in bacon fat until limp and transparent but not browned. Add flour and cook for 2 to 3 minutes.

Combine milk and tomato soup in a 3-quart saucepan; heat and stir until smooth. Combine all ingredients except bacon with tomato soup mixture. Heat and stir until slightly thickened. Garnish with crumbled bacon. Makes about 8 one-cup servings.

Corn Chowder

2 slices bacon, cooked and crumbled
1 small onion, chopped
1½ cups boiling water
1 package (10 ounces) frozen corn or 1 can
   (12 ounces) corn, undrained
½ teaspoon salt
Dash pepper
1 tall can evaporated milk
1 tablespoon butter
1 tablespoon flour

Cook the bacon slowly in large saucepan until crisp; remove and drain on paper towels. Add onions to pan and cook until transparent but not brown, about 10 minutes. Add boiling water, corn, seasonings, and milk.

Thicken with a roux made with blended butter and flour. Stir it to mix smoothly. Cook until thickened. Serve topped with crumbled bacon. Makes about 4 servings.

Clam Chowder

½ cup chopped onion
2 tablespoons butter or margarine
2 medium potatoes, diced
1 cup water
2 quarts milk
1 tablespoon chicken soup base
2 cans (about 7 ounces each) minced clams
    and juice
1 can (about 10 ounces) New England clam
    chowder
Roux (see page 12)
Dash garlic powder
½ teaspoon Worcestershire sauce

On low heat in heavy 4-quart pan, sauté onions in butter or margarine until soft but not brown (about 5 minutes). Add diced potatoes and 1 cup water. Cook until potatoes are tender, about 20 minutes. Add milk, soup base, clams and juice, and canned chowder. Heat. Thicken with a little roux and season with garlic powder, if desired. Add Worcestershire sauce. Taste to correct seasoning. Stir chowder while cooking to prevent it from burning. Makes about 3 quarts, 12 one-cup servings.

Crab Bisque

1 can (10½ ounces) each condensed cream of
    tomato, celery, mushroom, and green pea
    soups
5 cups milk (part cream, if desired)
1 or 2 cans crab meat
Salt
Pepper
Monosodium glutamate (MSG)
Parsley

Combine and blend soups. Heat milk; gradually add to soups, then add crab meat. Heat slowly, stirring constantly to prevent scorching. Season to taste; add chopped parsley. Makes 12 servings.

Canadian Cheese Soup

Ingredients	10 servings (2½ quarts)	60 servings (2½ gallons)
Chopped onions	½ cup	2 cups
Butter or margarine	¼ cup	1 cup
Flour	¼ cup	1 cup
Cornstarch	1½ tablespoons	6 tablespoons
Paprika	½ teaspoon	2 teaspoons
Salt	½ teaspoon	2 teaspoons
White pepper	¼ teaspoon	1 teaspoon
Milk, heated	1 quart	1 gallon
Chicken stock, heated	1 quart	1 gallon
Diced carrots, cooked	¾ cup	3 cups
Diced celery, cooked	¾ cup	3 cups
Shredded sharp Cheddar cheese	1 cup	1 quart
Chopped parsley	¼ cup	¾ cup

Sauté onion in melted butter until transparent but not brown (5 to 10 minutes). Add flour, cornstarch, paprika, salt, and pepper. Cook on low heat for about 10 minutes. Add milk and chicken stock and cook, stirring constantly, until thickened. Chop the cooked vegetables very fine, or mash slightly. Add them to milk mixture. Taste to correct seasonings. Just before serving, stir in shredded cheese and chopped parsley. Amount of vegetable may be increased if thicker soup is desired. Use 1 cup in the 10-serving recipe, 3½ to 4 cups in the large recipe.

Servings are based on one-cup amounts.

Washington Chowder

½ pound link sausages
4 cups water
¼ cup chopped onion
½ cup chopped celery
¾ cup cut-up carrots
1¾ cups frozen mixed vegetables
1 can red kidney beans
1 cup cooked tomatoes
⅓ cup cooked roast beef, chopped
3 beef bouillon cubes
1 teaspoon salt
½ teaspoon marjoram
⅛ teaspoon black pepper

Brown link sausages in a frying pan. Drain. Cool and cut into ¼-inch pieces. Place water in a large, heavy kettle. Add onion, celery, and carrots, and simmer until vegetables are tender, about 20 minutes. Add mixed vegetables, kidney beans, tomatoes, roast beef, and seasonings. Simmer for ½ hour to blend flavors. Add sausages just before serving. Makes 8 to 10 servings.

Lion House Chili

2 cups dry red Mexican beans
2 cans (8 ounces each) tomato sauce
2 cups tomato juice
1 tablespoon hot chili powder, or to taste
½ teaspoon cumin
2 teaspoons salt
½ teaspoon pepper
1 pound ground beef
1 cup chopped onion

Cover beans with cool water and soak overnight. Cook until tender. Add tomato sauce, tomato juice, and seasonings. Brown ground beef and onion in heavy skillet until lightly browned. Add to cooked bean mixture. Simmer for 1 hour or longer, stirring occasionally. Makes 10 to 12 servings.

Bean and Bacon Soup

¼ pound bacon
¼ cup chopped onion
1 quart water
1 can (about 10 ounces) bean and bacon soup
1½ cups cooked navy beans
Roux (see page 12)
Salt and pepper to taste

Sauté bacon; remove from pan and pour off fat. Measure 2 tablespoons bacon fat in a large, heavy kettle. Cook onion in bacon fat until soft but not brown (about 5 minutes). Add the water, soup, and beans. Bring to a boil; thicken with a little roux, if desired. Add salt and pepper to taste. Add cooked bacon and serve. Makes 2½ quarts, or 10 one-cup servings.

Split Pea Soup

1 pound (2 cups) split peas
8 cups water
1 cup chopped onion
1 cup chopped ham pieces, or meaty ham bone or hock
1 tablespoon salt
¼ teaspoon pepper
Roux, if desired

Combine all ingredients in a large soup kettle. Simmer for 1½ to 2 hours, or to desired consistency. Thicken slightly with a roux made with 2 tablespoons softened butter or margarine blended well with 2 tablespoons flour. Makes about 3 quarts, or 10 to 12 1-cup servings.

Meats

Rossini Tournedos

5 pound tenderloin of beef (center cut)
Salt and pepper
Melted butter

Cut raw beef into diagonal slices, about 1 inch thick, then cut each slice in half to make 2 small, thick steaks. Rub each slice with salt and pepper. Place them in a single layer in a shallow roasting pan. Brush with melted butter. Bake in a 450-degree F. oven about 10 minutes, without turning (or to desired doneness). Serve both halves of the slice on dinner plate with a generous spoonful of Bearnaise Sauce on one half, Bordelaise Sauce on the other half. Makes 10 servings.

Bordelaise Sauce

2 tablespoons butter
1 thin slice onion
2 tablespoons flour
1 cup beef broth
¼ teaspoon salt
⅛ teaspoon pepper
1 tablespoon chopped parsley
1 bay leaf, crushed
¼ teaspoon thyme

Heat butter in frying pan until golden brown. Add onion and cook until tender. Blend in flour and cook until it is deep brown. Remove from heat and stir in broth; stir and boil for 1 minute. Add salt, pepper, parsley, bay leaf, and thyme. Makes about 1 cup. Serve with beef tournedos.

Note: The addition of ¼ pound sliced mushrooms sautéed in 2 tablespoons butter makes an excellent variation.

Bearnaise Sauce

½ cup apple juice
2 tablespoons white vinegar
2 small green onions, chopped
1 tablespoon chopped parsley
1 teaspoon crushed dried tarragon
¼ teaspoon pepper
3 egg yolks, beaten
½ cup butter, melted
2 teaspoons lemon juice
¼ teaspoon salt
2 dashes cayenne pepper

Combine apple juice, vinegar, onions, parsley, tarragon, and pepper in a small heavy saucepan. Boil until mixture is reduced by half, or to about ½ cup. Add gradually to egg yolks, stirring well to blend. Return to heat and cook until thickened and creamy, stirring constantly. Beat in butter, lemon juice, salt, and cayenne pepper. Makes 1 cup. Serve with beef tournedos.

Chateaubriand
(Roast Beef Tenderloin)

5-pound tenderloin of beef, center cut
Garlic (optional)
Soft butter or 3 strips bacon
Salt

Trim excess fat or connective tissue from meat. Place meat in a shallow roasting pan. Rub with cut garlic and salt. Brush with soft butter or top with half strips of bacon. Bake in a 450-degree F. oven for 45 to 60 minutes (until meat is red to pink inside). Slit meat with tip of paring knife to check doneness. (Or use a meat thermometer and cook to desired doneness.)

Remove meat to a warm platter and slice ↗

on the diagonal in about ½-inch thick slices. Serve two slices per person, with Bearnaise Sauce or Bordelaise Sauce (recipes given above). Also good served with mushrooms, sliced and sautéed in butter. Makes about 10 servings.

Lamb Stew

    2 pounds lean lamb meat, cut in chunks
    2 tablespoons flour
    1½ teaspoons salt
    ¼ teaspoon pepper
    2 tablespoons cooking oil
    1 garlic clove, minced or pressed
    1 onion, finely chopped
    ½ cup thinly sliced celery
    ½ teaspoon dill weed
    2 cups water
    1½ teaspoons sugar
    1 cup sliced carrots
    1 cup green beans
    1 cup small white onions

Dredge lamb chunks in flour, salt, and pepper. Brown slightly in hot oil in dutch oven or large frying pan. Add garlic, onion, and celery to meat as it browns. Add dill weed and water; cover and simmer until meat is tender (about 2 hours). Add sugar and remaining vegetables, and simmer until they are tender, 10 to 15 minutes. Thicken liquid with a little additional flour mixed with cold water, if desired. Makes 6 to 8 servings. Good served with dumplings.

This recipe may also be made with leftover, cooked roast lamb. Follow directions for above except the cooked meat can simply be trimmed from the bone, cut in pieces, and warmed in leftover gravy, canned gravy, or gravy made from a mix. Cook and add vegetables and seasonings separately. Taste to correct seasonings.

Roast Beef
and Yorkshire Pudding

    Standing rib roast of beef (5 to 7 pounds)
    ½ teaspoon salt
    ⅛ teaspoon pepper

Wipe beef well with damp cloth. Rub the lean portion with salt and pepper. Insert a meat thermometer through the ouside fat into the thickest part of the muscle. Be careful that the tip does not touch a bone. Place in a shallow roasting pan in a 325-degree F. oven and cook until internal temperature reaches 140 degrees for rare (about 20 minutes a pound), 160 degrees for medium (about 25 minutes a pound), 170 degrees for well done (about 30 minutes a pound).

As soon as the roast is done, remove it from the oven to a warm platter and turn the oven temperature up to 425 degrees F. Keep meat warm while making pudding and gravy. Meat can be more easily sliced if it stands a while.

Yorkshire Pudding

    2 eggs
    1 cup milk
    1 cup sifted flour
    ½ teaspoon salt
    2 tablespoons roast beef drippings

Beat eggs, milk, flour, and salt until batter is smooth and creamy. Pour the 2 tablespoons drippings into a 10-inch pie pan. Tilt pan to coat with the fat. Pour in batter. Bake about 25 minutes, or until pudding is puffed and nicely browned. Serve immediately with the roast beef. Makes 8 servings.

Make gravy from the rest of the drippings, using roux to thicken as desired, and diluting with water or beef broth, if necessary.

Swiss Steak

6 cubed steaks, about 5 ounces each
¼ cup flour
1 tablespoon paprika
1 tablespoon cooking oil (more if needed)
½ package onion soup mix
1 cup canned tomatoes, drained and chopped
½ cup condensed tomato soup
½ cup beef gravy or 1 teaspoon beef soup base
1½ cups water

Pound steaks with combined flour and paprika. Brown quickly in hot oil. Combine remaining ingredients. Pour over browned, floured steaks in baking pan. Cover pan and bake at 300 degrees F. for 1 hour, or until tender. Remove cover the last 15 minutes. Boil down sauce so that it thickens slightly, if needed. Pour over steaks and serve. Makes 6 servings.

Beef Wellington

3½ to 4 pounds beef tenderloin
Pastry
8 ounces liver sausage or liver paté
1 egg, beaten slightly

Place meat on a rack in a shallow roasting pan and roast uncovered in a 425-degree F. oven for 20 to 30 minutes, rare to medium. Remove from oven and let stand for 30 minutes.

In the meantime, make Lion House Pastry for a 9-inch double crust pie. Or purchase puff pastry from the freezer case for patty shells. Pinch the individual shells together, then roll into an 18x14-inch rectangle, ¼-inch thick. Spread paté on pastry, then place cooked tenderloin lengthwise, top side down, in center of pastry. Bring the long sides of pastry up over the bottom of the tenderloin; brush with egg and seal the two sides together. Trim ends of pastry and fold over; brush with egg and seal. Carefully transfer the pastry-wrapped meat, seam side down, to a baking sheet. Cut decorative shapes from pastry trimmings and arrange on top. Brush egg over all.

Bake in a 425-degree F. oven for 30 minutes or until delicately browned. Let stand 10 minutes before carving. Makes 6 to 8 servings.

Party Swiss Steak

4 pounds beef round, top or bottom, cut about ½-inch thick
¾ cup flour
4 to 6 tablespoons shortening
1 tablespoon salt
¼ teaspoon pepper
½ teaspoon thyme
2 cups water
1 cup chopped celery
1 cup chopped green pepper
2 cans (1 pound each) tomatoes (about 4 cups)
½ pound mozzarella cheese, thinly sliced

Cut meat into serving-size pieces. Dredge with ½ cup flour. Brown in hot shortening. Remove meat to a large dutch oven or roasting pan. Blend remaining flour with hot drippings. Add seasonings. Gradually blend in water. Add vegetables. Cook and stir until slightly thickened.

Pour mixture over meat and bake at 325 degrees F. for 2½ to 3 hours, or until meat is tender. Top with slices of cheese. Return to oven just until cheese melts. Serve at once. Makes 8 to 10 servings.

Lion House Meat Loaf

2 pounds lean ground beef
1 teaspoon salt
3 eggs, beaten slightly
¾ cup dry bread crumbs
Sauce (below)

Mix ground beef, salt, eggs, bread crumbs, and half the sauce until well blended. Mold into one large or two small loaf pans. Bake at 350 degrees F. for 1½ hours for large loaf, about 1 hour for smaller ones. Remove from oven and allow to stand for about 10 minutes for easier slicing. Serve with remaining sauce. Makes 8 to 10 servings.

Sauce

½ cup chopped onion
2 tablespoons shortening
1 can (about 10½ ounces) tomato soup
1 teaspoon Worcestershire sauce
Few grains pepper
¼ cup water

Sauté onions in shortening until tender. Add soup, Worcestershire sauce, pepper, and water. Simmer a few minutes to blend flavors.

Beef Parmesan

6 cubed steaks
¼ cup evaporated milk
Dry bread crumbs
2 tablespoons cooking fat
Salt
½ cup Parmesan cheese
6 slices mozzarella cheese
1 can (15 ounces or about 2 cups) tomato sauce
1½ cups tomato juice
¼ cup water
½ teaspoon garlic powder
2 tablespoons chopped onions
Dash of thyme
Dash of pepper

Dip steaks in evaporated milk, then in bread crumbs; brown in hot fat. Remove from frying pan to a 9x13x2-inch baking pan. Sprinkle with salt and one-half of the Parmesan cheese. Place one slice mozzarella cheese on top of each steak. Combine remaining ingredients except Parmesan cheese in small saucepan. Heat, then pour over meat and cheese. Sprinkle with the remaining Parmesan cheese. Bake at 350 degrees F. for 30 minutes. Makes 6 servings.

Savory Steak Italia

1½ pounds round steak cut ¾ inch thick and cut into six serving portions
3 tablespoons flour
1 teaspoon salt
¼ teaspoon oregano
¼ teaspoon pepper, or to taste
1 can (15½ ounces) spaghetti sauce with mushrooms
1 package (9 ounces) frozen Italian green beans
1 can (6 ounces) whole onions, drained

Rub steak with ⅓ of a mixture of flour, salt, oregano, and pepper; reserve remainder of mixture for sauce. Cut steak into 6 pieces. In large skillet over medium heat, brown both sides of steak in small amount of hot cooking fat. Remove browned pieces to a shallow baking dish (about 11x7 inches).

Heat sauce and remaining flour mixture to boiling, stirring constantly. Pour over steak, cover, and bake in a 375 degree F. oven 45 minutes. Add vegetables; cover and bake another 45 minutes or until meat is tender. Makes 6 servings.

Stir-Fried Beef and Peppers

1 pound lean beef, cut in paper-thin strips (beef is easier to cut if partially frozen)
3 tablespoons soy sauce
1 tablespoon lemon juice
4 teaspoons cornstarch
¼ teaspoon sugar
⅛ teaspoon ground ginger
½ cup salad oil
½ pound mushrooms, thickly sliced
2 medium onions, quartered
2 small green peppers, cut in squares or strips
½ teaspoon salt

Combine meat strips with soy sauce, lemon juice, cornstarch, sugar, and ginger. Let stand while preparing vegetables.

Heat salad oil in large frying pan or dutch ⭧

Baked salmon steak, honeydew melon, green beans with slivered almonds, potatoes

oven. Stir-fry mushrooms, onions, green peppers, and salt until vegetables are tender crisp (about 5 minutes). Lift vegetables from the fat and reserve.

Stir-fry meat mixture in the hot oil until it loses its pink color (a minute or two). Add vegetables and stir until hot. Serve with cooked rice. Makes 4 to 6 servings.

Beef Stroganoff

1 clove garlic, cut in quarters
3 tablespoons olive oil or salad oil
1½ pounds lean round or sirloin steak, cut into thin bite-size strips (1 inch long x ¼ inch thick)
¼ to ⅓ cup chopped onion
¾ to 1 teaspoon salt
⅛ teaspoon pepper
½ pound fresh mushrooms, washed and sliced
¼ cup flour
1½ to 2 cups milk
½ to 1 teaspoon paprika
1 cup sour cream
Hot cooked rice

Heat garlic in oil in heavy skillet for a few minutes, then remove and discard garlic. Add meat to skillet; brown slightly. Add onion, salt, and pepper. Cover and cook slowly for 35 to 45 minutes or until meat is completely tender, turning occasionally. Add more oil or water during cooking, if necessary. Add mushrooms. Cover and cook gently until mushrooms are tender, about 10 minutes.

With slotted spoon, remove the meat and mushrooms to top of double boiler. Blend flour into drippings in pan. Slowly stir in milk. Cook and stir over medium heat until mixture thickens. Sprinkle in paprika until sauce is a light pinkish color. Add sauce to the meat and mushroom mixture in double boiler. Add sour cream. Mix and heat well before serving, but do not cook. Correct seasonings. Serve over rice. Makes about 5 cups, or 4 to 6 servings.

Beef and Seven Vegetables

1 tablespoon cooking oil
3 cups sliced cooked roast beef (about 1½x2-inch strips) or 1½ pounds fresh lean beef, cut into strips
2½ cups carrots, cut in thin circles
1½ cups sliced green pepper
1½ cups sliced onions
2½ cups slant-cut celery
1 can (about 4 ounces) bamboo shoots, drained
4 cups beef stock or 4 beef bouillon cubes and 4 cups water
½ to ¾ cup soy sauce
3 tablespoons cornstarch in ¼ cup cold water
15 cherry tomatoes
1 cup fresh or frozen snow peas
Cooked rice or Chinese noodles

Heat oil in frying pan. Add beef and brown lightly. Remove meat; add carrots and green pepper and stir-fry for 1 minute. Add onions and celery; stir-fry for 1 minute. Add bamboo shoots. Remove vegetables and keep warm. Vegetables should remain crisp as in Chinese cooking.

In heavy kettle, add soup stock and soy sauce. Bring to a gentle boil; thicken with cornstarch-water mixture. Add tomatoes, snow peas, vegetables, and meat, and heat gently. Serve in soup plates over boiled rice or Chinese noodles. Makes 8 servings.

Sweet and Sour Beef

1 pound tender lean beef, cut into thin strips*
1 tablespoon cooking oil
1 green pepper cut into ¼ inch strips
1 can (about 15 ounces) chunk pineapple, drained (reserve juice for sauce)
Hot cooked rice

Brown meat strips lightly in oil (do half and remove from pan, then do second half). Add sauce (below) and green pepper to meat strips and heat together until green pepper ↗

wilts but does not lose its color. Add pineapple chunks. Reheat and serve over cooked rice. Makes 6 servings.

Note: Meat is easier to cut if it is partially frozen.

Sauce

2 tablespoons cornstarch
6 tablespoons sugar
Pineapple juice with water added to make 1½ cups
3 tablespoons vinegar
2 tablespoons soy sauce (or to taste)

Mix cornstarch with sugar. Add pineapple-water, vinegar, and soy sauce. Boil together until thickened.

Ground Beef Stroganoff

½ cup chopped onion
1 small clove garlic, minced
1 tablespoon butter or margarine
1 pound ground beef
2 tablespoons flour
1 teaspoon salt
¼ teaspoon pepper
¼ teaspoon monosodium glutamate (MSG)
¼ teaspoon paprika
1 cup sliced mushrooms
1 can (about 10 ounces) cream of mushroom soup
1 cup sour cream
Cooked rice or noodles

Sauté onions and garlic in a little butter or margarine in a hot skillet. Stir in meat, flour, and seasonings, and sauté about 5 minutes or until meat loses its color. Add mushrooms, then soup. Simmer about 10 minutes. Stir in sour cream and heat, but do not boil. Add a little milk if needed. Season to taste. Serve on hot rice or noodles. Makes 4 to 6 servings.

Roulade of Beef

2 pounds top round of beef, cut ½-inch thick
Salt
Pepper
1 medium onion, finely chopped
1 small clove garlic, pressed or minced
¼ pound lean ground beef
¼ pound lean ground pork
¼ pound lean ground veal (optional)
1 tablespoon finely chopped parsley
1 slice bread soaked in ¼ cup milk
¼ teaspoon powdered cloves
½ teaspoon thyme
½ teaspoon salt
⅛ teaspoon pepper
3 tablespoons flour (about)
6 slices bacon
1 to 2 tablespoons cooking oil
2 medium onions, sliced
1 bay leaf
1 can (16 ounces) tomatoes and juice
1 cup chicken stock, or 1½ teaspoons chicken soup base and 1 cup water
2 tablespoons lemon juice
1 teaspoon sugar

Cut beef round into 6 pieces, about 2½x4 inches. Sprinkle each piece with salt and pepper. Pound with meat cleaver or rolling pin to flatten slightly.

Add chopped onion and garlic to ground beef, pork, and veal along with parsley, bread and milk, cloves, thyme, salt, and pepper. Mix well. Spoon a generous spoonful on each slice of round steak. Roll up jelly-roll fashion and fasten roll with skewers or toothpicks. Sprinkle each roll with flour, then wrap one slice bacon around each.

Brown roulades on all sides in hot oil in a 6-quart dutch oven. Add the 2 sliced onions and remaining ingredients to the pot. Cover pot, place in a 325-degree F. oven, and bake until roulades are fork tender, about 1½ hours.

Remove roulades to warm serving dish. Set pot on high heat and boil rapidly a few ↗

minutes to reduce sauce. Thicken, if necessary, with a little roux, 1 to 2 tablespoons. Taste to correct seasonings, then strain and pour over roulades. Makes 6 servings.

Stuffed Ground Beef

2 pounds lean ground beef
2 eggs, well beaten
1 cup dry bread crumbs
½ cup milk
2 teaspoons salt
¼ teaspoon pepper
2 cups herb stuffing mix
2 cans (10½ ounces each) cream of chicken soup
½ soup can water

Mix ground beef, eggs, bread crumbs, milk, salt, and pepper until well blended. Divide into 16 portions. Flatten into thin patties. Make up stuffing mix following package directions. Scoop about ¼ cup stuffing on 8 of the patties. Place a second pattie on top, then press around edges to seal well. Remove stuffed patties to a shallow baking pan. Brown in a 400-degree F. oven for about 25 minutes. Mix soup with water and pour over patties. Turn oven down to 350 degrees F. and continue baking for 30 minutes longer. To serve, spoon sauce remaining in baking pan over patties. Makes 8 servings.

Beef Goulash

2 pounds beef chuck cut into cubes about 1½ inches square
2 tablespoons oil (about)
2 large onions, chopped
½ cup canned tomato soup
2 bouillon cubes or 2 teaspoons soup base
1½ cups water
1 tablespoon paprika
1 teaspoon vinegar
Cooked noodles

Brown meat in a small amount of oil in skillet and remove when browned. Cook onions in

same skillet until golden brown. Add meat, tomato soup, bouillon cubes, water, paprika, and vinegar and stir to mix. Lower heat and simmer about 2 hours or until meat is very tender. Serve with noodles. Makes 4 to 6 hearty servings. Can also be cooked in a slow cooker, on low heat, 6 to 8 hours.

Beef Enchiladas

Sauce

3 cans (8 ounces each) tomato sauce
1 can (1 pound) chili con carne without beans
1 can (1 pound) kidney beans, ground
3 cups tomato juice
1 teaspoon basil
1 teaspoon chili powder
1 teaspoon oregano
½ teaspoon crushed red peppers

Mix all ingredients together in saucepan. Simmer on low heat for 30 minutes.

Filling

1 pound lean ground beef
½ cup tomato sauce
1 tablespoon taco seasoning
1 teaspoon crushed red pepper
2 teaspoons oregano
Dash of Tabasco sauce
12 corn tortillas
1 cup grated Cheddar cheese
¼ cup ground onions

Brown ground beef in skillet. Add tomato sauce, taco seasoning, red pepper, oregano, and Tabasco sauce. Mix thoroughly. Divide beef mixture and spoon onto each corn tortilla. Sprinkle cheese and ground onions over the beef mixture and roll up tortillas. Place seam side down in baking dish. Pour sauce over top. Bake at 350 degrees F. for 30 minutes. Sprinkle with additional cheese just before serving. Makes 12 enchiladas.

Shepherd's Pie

1 can (about 10 ounces) gravy, or use leftover
    gravy
1 cup left-over roast lamb or beef*
¾ cup sliced carrots, parboiled
½ cup chopped onions, parboiled
½ cup chopped celery, parboiled
½ cup frozen peas
Salt and pepper to taste
3 potatoes, boiled, drained, and mashed, or use
    dehydrated potato flakes or granules to make
    3 cups mashed potatoes
½ cup grated cheese

Combine gravy, meat, carrots, onions, celery, and peas. Correct seasonings. Place mixture in an 8x8-inch baking pan. "Frost" top with mashed potatoes; sprinkle with cheese. Heat in 350-degree F. oven until cheese melts and mixture bubbles. Makes 6 servings.

You may use raw meat, one-half pound of either beef or lamb cubes. Brown well in a little cooking oil, then add water to cover; add the carrots, onions, and celery after the meat has simmered about 1 hour. Cook until meat and vegetables are tender. Thicken this mixture with a little flour and water thickening (about 2 tablespoons flour shaken in a ½-pint jar with ½ cup cold water). Proceed as above.

Orange Glaze
for Ham

1 can (6 ounces) frozen orange juice
¼ cup firmly packed brown sugar
½ teaspoon dry mustard
1 teaspoon Worcestershire sauce

Combine ingredients and heat, stirring constantly, until sugar dissolves. (This makes about 1 cup, or enough sauce to glaze a 6- to 7-pound ham.)

Place ham in a large shallow baking pan. Bake in 350-degree F. oven, allowing 15 to 20 minutes per pound. After 30 minutes baking, spread top generously with orange glaze. Continue baking, basting every 10 minutes with more orange glaze, 1 hour longer, or until meat is richly glazed.

Mustard Sauce
for Ham

3 egg yolks, slightly beaten
½ cup brown sugar
1 tablespoon flour
¼ cup dry mustard
½ cup vinegar
½ cup water
¼ cup margarine

To egg yolks in small saucepan add well-combined dry ingredients. Mix well. Add vinegar and water. Cook over low heat until thickened, stirring constantly. Add margarine and remove from heat. Stir well and cool. Makes 2 cups. Leftover sauce will keep in refrigerator several weeks.

Apple 'n' Orange
Pork Chops

8 pork chops, about ½-inch thick
Salt and pepper
1 tablespoon shortening
½ cup chopped onion
1 cup uncooked rice (not the quick-cooking
    kind)
1½ cups water
1 cup peeled and chopped tart apple
1 cup orange sections
1½ teaspoons salt
⅛ teaspoon pepper
⅛ teaspoon poultry seasoning (optional)

Trim excess fat from pork chops; season lightly with salt and pepper. Brown quickly in shortening. Pour from skillet all but 2 tablespoons of the drippings. Sauté onion in the 2 tablespoons fat. Combine all remaining ingredients except pork chops with the onion; mix well, then pour into a greased 2- or 3-quart shallow casserole (9x13x2-inch). Arrange chops on this mixture. Cover and bake at 350 degrees F. about 45 minutes.

This recipe is also very good without the apple or the oranges, or without both. Makes 8 servings.

Porcupine Meatballs

1 pound lean ground beef
⅓ cup uncooked rice
¼ cup chopped onion
¼ cup water
1 teaspoon salt
Dash pepper
1 can (10½ ounces) condensed tomato soup
½ teaspoon chili powder
½ cup water

Combine beef, rice, onion, water, salt, and pepper. Shape into about 15 one-inch balls. Blend soup and chili powder; stir in ½ cup water; bring to boil, and add meatballs. Cover and simmer gently for one hour, stirring occasionally. Makes about 6 servings.

Beef Pasties

Pastry for a 9-inch 2-crust pie
1 pound lean ground beef
1 small can mushrooms, undrained
½ cup chopped onions
½ cup chopped celery
3 tablespoons sweet pickle relish
1 can (10½ ounces) cream of mushroom soup
1 can (about 10 ounces) beef gravy or use
    leftover gravy

Roll out pastry dough and cut 12 circles each 5 inches in diameter. Combine ground beef, mushrooms, onion, and celery in frying pan and cook until tender. Add pickle relish and soup. Mix well. Place a scoop of meat mixture (about ½ cup) in center of each of 6 pastry circles. Top with remaining 6 circles. Press circles together with fingers or a fork to seal. Prick top with fork. Bake at 400 degrees F. for 30 minutes. Serve with beef gravy. Makes 6 servings.

Sweet and Sour Meatballs

1 to 1½ pounds lean ground beef
¾ cup rolled oats
2 eggs, slightly beaten
½ cup finely chopped onion
½ cup milk
1 teaspoon salt
Few grains pepper
1 teaspoon Worcestershire sauce

Combine all ingredients; mix well. Form into about 12 balls, each about 2 inches in diameter. Place in casserole dish. Cover with sauce (below). Bake at 350 degrees F. for about 30 minutes. Makes 6 to 8 servings, 2 large meatballs each.

Sauce

½ cup brown sugar
¼ cup vinegar
1 teaspoon prepared mustard
¼ cup barbeque sauce
1 teaspoon Worcestershire sauce

Combine ingredients and blend thoroughly. Heat and pour over meatballs.

Ham with Maple Syrup and Cider Glaze

1 cup maple syrup
½ cup sweet cider
Ham
Whole cloves

Combine syrup and cider and set aside. Place ham in roasting pan, fat side up. Score fat with a sharp knife, diagonally, in two directions. Stud with whole cloves the diamonds formed by scoring. Brush entire surface with syrup and cider glaze. Bake at 325 degrees F., basting occasionally with the glaze. Bake a fully cooked ham for 15 to 20 minutes per pound to develop flavor and tenderness.

Easy Lasagna Casserole

½ pound regular noodles (about ½-inch wide)
½ to 1 pound lean ground beef
¼ cup chopped onion
1 clove garlic, minced
1 tablespoon salad oil
1 can (8 ounces) tomato sauce
3 cups tomato juice
1 teaspoon sugar
1 teaspoon salt
¼ teaspoon basil
¼ teaspoon rosemary
2 teaspoons oregano
1 teaspoon chili powder
1 tablespoon Italian seasoning
½ teaspoon fennel seed (optional)
2 tablespoons Parmesan cheese
2 cups shredded sharp Cheddar cheese

Cook noodles in boiling salted water until just tender, about 10 minutes. While noodles cook, sauté meat, onion, and garlic in hot salad oil until meat loses its color. Add drained noodles and all remaining ingredients except Cheddar cheese.

Pour into a 9x13-inch casserole. Cover with foil and bake 45 minutes at 325 degrees F. Remove foil. Spread top with shredded cheese and bake another 30 minutes, uncovered. Makes 8 to 10 servings.

Fruit Sauce for Ham

3 cups pineapple juice
1 can (6 ounces) frozen orange juice concentrate
¾ cup brown sugar
1 tablespoon cornstarch

Combine ingredients; heat and stir in heavy saucepan until slightly thickened. Pour over ham and bake. This can also be ladled over ham at the time of serving. Makes about 1 quart.

Macaroni and Beef Bake

2 tablespoons cooking oil
2 pounds ground beef (use fresh meat or leftover roast beef, ground)
⅔ cup finely chopped onion
⅓ pound (1 cup) macaroni
4 cups tomato juice
1 can (10½ ounces) tomato soup
1½ cups shredded Cheddar cheese
1½ teaspoons chili powder
Few grains of salt and pepper

In frying pan in hot oil brown ground beef, onion, and macaroni. Add tomato juice, tomato soup, one-half of the cheese, chili powder, salt, and pepper.

Bake in a large casserole at 350 degrees F. for about 1 hour or until macaroni is tender. Cover with cheese and return to oven until cheese melts. Makes 8 servings.

Buffet Ham

1 boneless ham (7 or 8 pounds)
Mustard
1½ cups orange juice
1½ cups maple syrup
1 teaspoon allspice
½ teaspoon mace
½ teaspoon cinnamon
2 teaspoons paprika
3 cups cream (part whipping cream, part half-and-half)

Have butcher cut ham in ½-inch slices. Spread one side of each ham slice generously with prepared mustard. Arrange in large roasting pan, slices overlapping. Combine next six ingredients and pour over ham. Bake uncovered ½ hour at 350 degrees F. Remove from oven and pour on the combined creams. Return to oven and bake about 1 hour longer. Spoon hot sauce over each slice as it is served. Makes about 16 servings.

Party Ham Roll-Ups

25 slices ham (about 5 pounds)
25 slices Swiss cheese (about 1½ pounds)
Cornbread Stuffing (below)
Apricot Sauce (below)

Lay out ham and cheese slices. Spoon about ⅓ cup Cornbread Stuffing in center of each ham slice. Lay slice of Swiss cheese on top of stuffing. Roll up and secure with toothpick. Place in shallow baking dish. Bake for 45 minutes at 350 degrees F. Spoon about 2 or 3 tablespoons sauce over each roll-up when serving. Makes 25 servings. (Recipe may be halved, if desired.)

Cornbread Stuffing

1 pan cornbread (8x8-inch), any favorite recipe
   or package mix
1 cup finely chopped celery and leaves
4 tablespoons finely chopped onion
1 cup butter or margarine
½ cup apricot preserves
¼ cup water

Cook celery and onion in margarine until soft. Stir in preserves and water. Toss this mixture lightly with crumbled cornbread. Add more water, if desired, for a stuffing that is more moist.

Apricot Sauce

1 tablespoon cornstarch
2 tablespoons brown sugar
1 cup water
1 cup pineapple juice
1 tablespoon butter
¼ cup apricot preserves

Mix cornstarch and brown sugar in small saucepan. Add water and pineapple juice, and stir over medium heat until mixture boils and is thickened. Stir in butter and preserves.

Ham and Green Noodle Casserole

1 cup sour cream
1 can (10½ ounces) Cheddar cheese soup
2 cups (6 ounces) uncooked green noodles,
   cooked and drained (recipe below)
1½ cups cooked, diced ham
½ cup pitted ripe olives, sliced
1 can (2½ ounces) mushrooms, drained
¾ teaspoon prepared mustard
¼ cup milk
⅛ teaspoon pepper
1 cup grated sharp Cheddar cheese

Combine sour cream and soup. Beat till smooth. Add remaining ingredients except cheese. Place in shallow baking pan (8x8x2-inch) or casserole. Sprinkle with grated cheese. Bake at 350 degrees F. for 25 minutes. Makes 8 servings.

Green Noodles

1 package (10 ounces) frozen chopped spinach
2 eggs
½ teaspoon salt
2½ cups flour (about)

Cook spinach according to package directions. Drain well, pressing out moisture with back of spoon. Force spinach through food mill or buzz in a blender. In mixing bowl beat eggs and salt. Beat in spinach purée. Add flour, enough to make a firm dough. Knead thoroughly. Cut dough into 4 pieces and let them rest 30 minutes.

Roll each piece of dough very thinly on a floured board into a 12-inch square. Remove each square as rolled to a kitchen towel and let dry about 1 hour. Cut into strips about ¼-inch wide.

Cook noodle strips in a large quantity of boiling salted water 8 to 10 minutes. Drain and rinse thoroughly. Makes about 1 pound noodles.

Barbecued Spareribs

3 to 4 pounds pork spareribs
1 tablespoon salt
½ teaspoon black pepper
2 onions, chopped
2 tablespoons vinegar
1 teaspoon chili powder
2 tablespoons Worcestershire sauce
¾ cup water
½ teaspoon cayenne pepper
¾ cup catsup
1 teaspoon paprika

Sprinkle spareribs with salt and pepper. Place in a roaster and cover with onions. To make sauce, combine remaining ingredients and pour over meat. Cover and bake at 350 degrees F. about 2 hours. Baste and turn ribs once or twice. Uncover last half hour for browning. Makes 6 servings.

Stuffed Pork Chops

6 pork chops, 1-inch thick
½ cup finely chopped onion
½ cup finely chopped celery
¼ cup butter
1 cup chicken stock
1 teaspoon salt
1 teaspoon each poultry seasoning and sage
3 cups ground dry bread crumbs
1 can cream of celery soup
⅓ can water

Have butcher cut a pocket-slit in each pork chop. Sauté onion and celery in butter. Mix in stock and seasonings. Remove from heat and mix in bread crumbs until moistened. Stuff each pork chop with ½ cup stuffing. Coat each chop with a breading mixture of fine bread crumbs, salt, pepper, and paprika. Place chops in shallow baking dish. Combine celery soup and water and pour over chops. Bake 1½ to 2 hours in a 350-degree F. oven. Makes 6 servings.

Sweet and Sour Pork

2 pounds lean pork, about ½-inch thick
2 tablespoons cornstarch
¼ cup soy sauce
3 tablespoons oil
2 cups carrots cut in diagonal chunks
3 small onions, cut in quarters
1 green pepper, cut in strips
1 can (20 ounces) chunk pineapple, drained
3 tablespoons cornstarch
2 tablespoons sugar
2 cups liquid (drained juice from pineapple plus water)
⅔ cup vinegar
½ cup soy sauce
Cooked rice

Cut pork into 2-inch strips. Mix 2 tablespoons cornstarch and ¼ cup soy sauce, and marinate pork in this mixture for an hour or two, or overnight, in refrigerator. Drain (save marinade). Stir-fry meat in hot oil until evenly browned and tender (about 10 minutes). Remove meat from pan. Stir-fry carrots and onions in same pan, using more oil, if necessary. Cover and cook on low heat until tender crisp, about 10 minutes. Add green pepper and pineapple. Return meat to pan, then stir in marinade.

In the meantime, make the sauce: Mix 3 tablespoons cornstarch and the sugar in a small saucepan. Add 2 cups liquid, vinegar, and ½ cup soy sauce. Stir and cook until thickened and clear. Pour over meat and vegetables, and heat until flavors are blended, about 10 minutes. Taste to correct seasonings. Serve over cooked rice. Makes 8 to 10 servings.

Pork
Chow Mein

1 pound lean pork, cubed
Oil
1 cup chopped onion
1 cup slant-cut celery
½ cup canned sliced bamboo shoots
1 small can mushrooms
1 cup bean sprouts
1 cup chicken soup stock
½ teaspoon sugar
2 tablespoons soy sauce
1½ tablespoons cornstarch
Chow mein noodles or hot cooked rice

Stir-fry cubed pork in oiled frying pan until browned and cooked tender. Remove meat from pan. Add vegetables and more oil, if necessary, and stir-fry for about 5 minutes. (Do not overcook—vegetables should be crisp.) Combine the meat and vegetables; mix well.

Heat chicken stock, sugar, and soy sauce. Make a paste of cornstarch and a little cold water; stir into the hot stock mixture. Cook, stirring constantly, until thickened. Pour over meat and vegetables. Let the chow mein and sauce have time to blend flavors before serving. Serve over chow mein noodles or rice. Makes 4 to 6 servings.

Green Sauce

1 cup parsley, packed
1 or 2 cloves garlic
1 teaspoon grated Parmesan cheese
1 teaspoon salt
½ cup olive oil

Blend all ingredients in blender until smooth. Split small loaf of French bread lengthwise and spread with sauce. Broil until bubbly. For spaghetti sauce, add 2 tablespoons Green Sauce to meat sauce recipe.

Ham Loaf
with Mustard Sauce

2 pounds ground pork
1 pound ground ham
1 egg, beaten
1½ cups milk
¼ teaspoon salt
1 cup dry bread crumbs or soda cracker crumbs
3 tablespoons tomato soup
½ teaspoon paprika
2 tablespoons chopped onion
2 tablespoons chopped green pepper
Onion slices

Have butcher grind pork and ham together. Mix all ingredients and place in buttered 9x5-inch loaf pan, putting onion slices on top. Bake at 350 degrees F. for 1½ hours. Serve with Mustard Sauce. Makes 8 to 10 servings.

Mustard Sauce

½ cup tomato soup
½ cup vinegar
¼ pound butter
½ cup prepared mustard
½ cup sugar
3 egg yolks

Combine all ingredients and cook slowly until thick, on low heat. Serve on ham loaf. Makes about 2½ cups.

Mint Sauce
for Lamb

½ cup vinegar
1 to 2 tablespoons sugar
¼ cup chopped fresh mint leaves

Scald vinegar; add sugar and stir until dissolved. Add the mint and allow the sauce to brew for an hour or more before serving.

Stuffed Pork Chops

Ham-Cheese Strata

8 slices firm white bread, crusts removed
4 slices sharp Cheddar cheese
1 cup chopped cooked ham
4 eggs, beaten
2 cups milk
1 teaspoon finely chopped onion
Dash pepper
½ teaspoon salt
¼ teaspoon dry mustard

Arrange 4 slices of bread in bottom of an 8-inch square baking pan. Cover with slices of cheese, ham, and remaining bread. Combine eggs, milk, onion, and seasonings; pour over sandwiches. Let stand 1 hour. Bake in 325-degree F. oven 1 hour or until lightly browned and puffy. Let stand a few minutes; cut into squares. Makes 4 to 6 servings.

Mustard Ring

¾ cup sugar
½ teaspoon salt
2 tablespoons dry mustard
½ cup vinegar
½ cup water
4 eggs, well beaten
1 envelope gelatin
1 tablespoon cold water
½ teaspoon horseradish
1½ cups whipping cream, whipped

Combine sugar, salt, and dry mustard. Add vinegar, water, and eggs. Soak gelatin in cold water and dissolve over hot water. Add to egg mixture and cook until creamy. Cook on low heat, stirring constantly. Add horseradish. Fold in whipped cream. Pour into 4-cup ring mold and chill until set. Serve on buffet with baked ham or roast beef.

Oriental Rice

Ingredients	10 servings	20 servings
Bacon	¼ pound	½ pound
Onions, diced	1 cup	2 cups
Diced carrots	½ cup	1 cup
Diced celery	¾ cup	1½ cups
Green pepper, diced	1 small	1 large
Cooked meat, diced	2 cups	4 cups
Soy sauce	3 tablespoons	6 tablespoons
Cold cooked rice	3 cups	6 cups

In a large skillet, cook bacon until crisp; remove from skillet. Add onions and stir-fry one minute. Add carrots and stir-fry one minute. Add celery and green pepper and stir-fry one minute. Add meat and soy sauce and heat through.

Break up cold cooked rice. Stir gently into meat and vegetables, taking care that each grain of rice is coated with oil and liquids that have formed in the pan. Heat through; add crumbled bacon and serve immediately.

Noodles Romanoff

2 packages (8 ounces each) noodles
3 cups large-curd cottage cheese
2 garlic cloves, mashed
2 teaspoons Worcestershire sauce
2 cups commercial sour cream
1 bunch green onions, chopped
½ teaspoon Tabasco sauce
1 cup grated Parmesan cheese

Cook noodles as package directs. Drain. Combine with all other ingredients. Pour into a buttered 2- to 3-quart casserole. Bake at 350 degrees F. for 25 minutes. Makes about 16 servings.

Note: Ingredients may be prepared ahead of time, then refrigerated. Allow an additional 15 minutes' cooking time.

Poultry

Baked Chicken Supreme

4 whole chicken breasts, halved*
¼ cup shortening (about)
1 small garlic clove
⅓ cup chopped onion
1½ teaspoons salt
½ teaspoon sugar
½ teaspoon oregano (optional)
¼ cup flour
1 cup tomato juice
1 can (about 10½ ounces) tomato soup
1 cup sour cream
¼ cup milk
2 tablespoons grated Parmesan cheese
Hot cooked rice

Brown chicken breasts in shortening. Use more shortening if needed. Remove from frying pan and place in 9x9x2-inch baking dish. Pour off all but 2 tablespoons of the drippings. Add garlic and onion to skillet; cover and cook until soft but not brown (about 5 minutes). Blend in salt, sugar, oregano, and flour. Add tomato juice and tomato soup; heat to boiling, stirring constantly. Remove from heat and blend in sour cream. Stir vigorously. Add milk to thin sauce a bit (add a little more if needed). Add Parmesan cheese. Pour over chicken in baking dish. Cover and bake at 325 degrees F. for about 45 minutes, or until meat is fork tender. Serve with cooked rice. Makes 8 servings.

Skinned and boned breasts are a little nicer, but unskinned, unboned pieces may be used. Or use all the pieces from one chicken, or the pieces desired from two chickens.

Chicken Royale

4 whole chicken breasts, halved
2 tablespoons butter
¼ cup chopped onion
¼ pound fresh mushrooms
2 tablespoons flour
1 cup light cream
1 cup sour cream
1 teaspoon lemon juice
8 slices cooked ham
½ of a small package of stuffing mix, made up by package directions (or make your own, using any favorite recipe for about 2 cups of stuffing)

Skin and bone each chicken breast half. Flatten each piece, skinned side down, between pieces of plastic wrap to about ⅛-inch thickness, using a meat mallet or rolling pin.

In large frying pan, melt butter, then cook onions and mushrooms, covered, until soft but not brown, about 10 minutes. Remove from pan and reserve.

In same pan, brown flattened chicken breasts. Add a little more butter, or cooking oil, if needed. Remove chicken pieces from pan and reserve.

Add flour to pan drippings and blend well. Gradually add the light cream and sour cream. Heat well but do not boil, stirring constantly until mixture thickens. Add reserved onions and mushrooms, and lemon juice. Taste to correct seasonings.

Grease a 9x13x2-inch baking dish. Cut ham slices to fit chicken breasts, and place each ham slice in baking pan. Top ham slices with about ¼ cup stuffing; then cover with chicken breast.

Pour sauce mix over all. Heat in 325-degree F. oven for about one-half hour, or until hot and bubbly and chicken is fork tender. Makes 8 servings.

Easy Chicken Bake

Salt
Garlic salt
Paprika
1 fryer, cut up or 6 good-sized pieces of chicken
1 can (10½ ounces) cream of mushroom soup
1 cup cream or ¾ cup evaporated milk
Chopped parsley

Mix salt, garlic salt, and paprika. Thoroughly rub mixture into chicken pieces. Spread chicken in one layer in a shallow baking dish or pan. Dilute the soup with cream and pour over the chicken; sprinkle with parsley. Bake uncovered at 350 degrees F. for 1½ hours. Makes 6 servings.

Chicken Kiev

1 cup butter or margarine
1½ teaspoons salt
⅛ teaspoon pepper
¼ cup chopped chives
¼ cup minced parsley
3 chicken breasts, skinned, boned, and halved
2 eggs
½ cup orange juice
4 tablespoons flour
1 cup bread crumbs
½ teaspoon grated orange rind

Blend butter, salt, pepper, chives, and parsley. Form into 6 finger-size strips. Place on pan and put in freezer until very firm.

Flatten chicken breast pieces between layers of waxed paper. Set aside. Make batter with eggs, orange juice, and flour; beat together until smooth. Heat, stirring constantly, until slightly thickened. Set aside.

Wrap a butter finger in each flattened chicken breasts, making a roll. Tuck the ends inside as you roll. Dip rolls in batter, then roll in combined bread crumbs and orange rind. Bake in a 375-degree F. oven for 45 minutes. Makes 6 servings. Serve with Mushroom Sauce.

Mushroom Sauce

¾ pound fresh mushrooms, washed, sliced, and sprinkled with flour
3 tablespoons butter
1 cup light cream

Cook mushrooms in butter until they give up their juice, about 5 minutes. Add cream and stir until the mixture thickens. Taste for seasoning. Serve hot over Chicken Kiev.

Chicken Alabam

8 pieces chicken
⅓ cup flour
½ teaspoon paprika
½ teaspoon salt
Dash of pepper
Dash of thyme
5 tablespoons butter
¼ cup onion, chopped
1 cup chicken soup stock*
½ cup light cream
¼ teaspoon lemon juice
2 tablespoons pimiento

Dredge chicken pieces with mixture of flour, paprika, salt, pepper, and thyme. Brush chicken with 3 tablespoons melted butter and brown in oven, or shake off excess flour and sauté in about 3 tablespoons cooking oil.

Sauté onion lightly in 2 tablespoons butter for 5 minutes. Stir in excess flour from dredging chicken. Add soup stock. Cook and stir until thickened. Add light cream and cook until smooth and thick. Add lemon juice, then pimiento; blend well. Pour sauce over chicken in a 2- to 3-quart casserole; cover and bake 1¼ hours at 325 degrees F., or until chicken is fork tender. Serve over cooked rice. Makes 4 to 6 servings (makes 8 servings if chicken breasts only are used—one-half breast for each serving).

*Or use 2 chicken bouillon cubes, or 1½ teaspoons chicken soup base granules and 1 cup water.

Chicken and Cashews

2 pounds chicken breasts
¼ cup cornstarch
2 tablespoons soy sauce
1 cup oil
2 cups chicken broth or chicken stock
2 tablespoons cornstarch
1 tablespoon cold water
½ cup cashews

Remove bones and skin from chicken breasts. Cut chicken into bite-size cubes. Roll in ¼ cup cornstarch, then in soy sauce. Place on a tray to air dry. In a heavy skillet, heat oil to 375 degrees F. Fry chicken pieces in hot oil till golden brown. Drain well.

Bring chicken broth to a boil and thicken with a mixture of 2 tablespoons cornstarch and 1 tablespoon cold water. Season to taste and simmer for 15 minutes. Just before serving, add chicken and cashews. Serve over Oriental Rice (page 36). Makes 6 servings.

Chicken and Broccoli Bake

4 chicken breast halves
3 packages (10 ounces each) frozen broccoli cooked according to package directions, or 2 pounds fresh broccoli, well trimmed and cooked until tender crisp
1 can (10½ ounces) cream of chicken soup
½ cup milk
½ cup mayonnaise
1 cup grated Cheddar cheese
1 teaspoon lemon juice
½ cup buttered crumbs

Simmer chicken breasts in water just to cover for about 30 minutes, or until tender. (You may add a bay leaf, ½ medium onion, sliced, and a sliced stalk of celery to season the stock for another use.) Remove chicken from broth and cool enough to handle. Then remove skin and bones and slice or break into large pieces.

In a 9x9x2-inch pan, arrange broccoli with flowerettes pointed out toward edge of pan. Lay chicken meat over broccoli. Make a sauce by combining soup, milk, and mayonnaise and stir until smooth. Add cheese and lemon juice. Pour sauce over chicken and broccoli to cover chicken pieces completely. Cover pan with aluminum foil and bake at 350 degrees F. for about 30 minutes. Sprinkle crumbs on top after chicken is heated through or just before serving. Makes 5 to 6 servings.

Chicken Porter Rockwell

1 recipe Lion House Pie Dough
8 boneless chicken breasts
4 tablespoons butter
4 tablespoons minced green onions
2 cups finely chopped mushrooms
1 teaspoon minced garlic
1 tablespoon chopped parsley
Salt and pepper
1 egg, beaten
½ teaspoon salt

Prepare pie dough according to instructions. Roll out and cut into 16 circles each 5 inches in diameter.

Flatten chicken breasts with a meat mallet until ¼-inch thick. Prepare filling by melting butter in a heavy frying pan. Add onions, mushrooms, and garlic, and sauté until onions are tender. Add parsley and season with salt and pepper. Place a heaping tablespoon of the mushroom mixture on each chicken breast. Roll up, tuck in ends, and place each breast on a pastry circle. Place second pastry circle on top, sealing outside edge by pressing them together with a fork. Beat egg and ½ teaspoon salt, and brush on each pastry; cut vent in top. Place on a greased cookie sheet. Bake 25 minutes at 400 degrees F. Serve with chicken gravy or a clear chicken glaze. Makes 8 servings.

Savory Chicken in Sauce

8 small whole chicken breasts, skinned and
    boned
8 thin slices corned beef
8 strips bacon
2 cans (10½ ounces each) cream of mushroom
    soup
1 pint sour cream

Lay chicken breasts flat and pound to flatten slightly. In center of each breast place one slice corned beef. Fold breast loosely, then wrap with bacon strip. Place the eight rolls in a shallow (9x13-inch) baking dish. Combine well the soup and sour cream (thin slightly with a little milk, if desired), and pour over chicken rolls. Bake at 325 degrees F. for about 2 hours, or until chicken is fork tender. Makes 8 servings.

Orange Chicken

½ cup flour
2 teaspoons salt
¼ teaspoon pepper
2 fryers, cut up
⅓ cup butter, melted
1 onion, thinly sliced
1 can (6 ounces) frozen orange juice concentrate
1 juice can of water
¼ cup brown sugar
½ teaspoon nutmeg
2 tablespoons cornstarch

Combine flour, salt, and pepper in a plastic bag. Add chicken pieces and shake to coat well. Brush each piece with butter. Place chicken pieces in a baking pan, skin side up, and brown in a 400-degree F. oven. Remove chicken to a 2-quart casserole and spread onions generously over surface.

Combine orange juice, water, brown sugar, nutmeg, and cornstarch. Pour over chicken. Cover with foil and bake at 325 degrees F. for 1 hour or until fork tender. Makes 6 to 8 servings.

Chicken Cordon Bleu

4 whole chicken breasts, halved
8 thin slices cooked ham (baked or boiled ham
    slices may be used)
4 slices Swiss cheese, cut into fingers about 1½
    inches long and ½ inch thick
Salt
Pepper
Thyme or rosemary
¼ cup melted butter or margarine
½ cup cornflake crumbs

Skin and bone chicken breast halves. Place each half between sheets of plastic wrap, skinned side down, and pound with meat mallet to about ⅛-inch thickness.

On each ham slice place a finger of cheese. Sprinkle lightly with seasonings. Roll ham and cheese jelly-roll style, then roll each chicken breast with ham and cheese inside. Tuck in ends and seal well. (Tie rolls if necessary, or fasten edges with toothpicks.) Dip each roll in melted butter, then roll in cornflake crumbs, turning to thoroughly coat each roll.

Place rolls in a 9x13x2-inch baking dish. Bake, uncovered, in a 400-degree F. oven for about 40 minutes, or until chicken is golden brown. Serve with Cordon Bleu Sauce, if desired. Makes 6 to 8 servings.

Cordon Bleu Sauce

1 can (10½ ounces) cream of chicken soup
½ cup sour cream
1 teaspoon lemon juice

Blend ingredients and heat. Serve over chicken rolls, if desired. Makes about 2 cups, 8 servings of ¼ cup each.

Chicken Taco Pie

1 cup chopped onions
2 tablespoons cooking oil
2 tablespoons taco seasoning, or to taste
1¾ teaspoons chili powder
1 teaspoon salt
¼ teaspoon pepper
3 cans (10½ ounces) cream of mushroom soup
1½ cups sour cream
3 cups cubed cooked chicken
6 to 8 tortillas
1 cup Monterey Jack cheese, shredded

In a skillet, cook onions in oil until tender but not brown. Add seasonings, cream of mushroom soup, and sour cream; heat and stir until smooth and warm. Add chicken.

Oil a 2- to 3-quart flat casserole and cover the bottom with torn-up oiled tortillas. Spread half of chicken mixture on tortillas; top with additional oiled tortillas, then cover with remaining filling. Sprinkle with shredded cheese. Bake in a 350-degree F. oven until hot and bubbly. Makes 6 to 8 servings.

Quiche Lorraine

1 9-inch unbaked pie crust
1 cup (4 ounces) shredded Swiss cheese
6 slices bacon, cooked and crumbled
¾ cup ham, minced
2 green onions, sliced and chopped
½ green pepper, chopped
3 eggs, slightly beaten
1 cup light cream
½ teaspoon grated lemon peel
½ teaspoon salt
¼ teaspoon dry mustard

Bake unpricked pastry shell for 5 minutes at 425 degrees F. Remove from oven and arrange cheese, bacon, and ham in bottom of shell. Sprinkle with green onion and green pepper.

In medium bowl combine eggs, cream, lemon peel, salt, and dry mustard. Pour evenly over cheese mixture. Bake at 325 degrees F. for 45 minutes or until set. Remove from heat and let stand about ten minutes before serving. Cut pie into 6 servings.

Bread Stuffing

Ingredients	For Chicken (4-pound size)	For Turkey (12-16 pounds)
Butter or margarine	⅓ cup	1 cup
Chopped onion	3 to 4 tablespoons	¾ to 1 cup
Finely chopped celery (optional)	¾ to 1 cup	2 cups
Stale bread cubes	1 quart	3 to 4 quarts
Salt	1 teaspoon	1 tablespoon
Pepper	⅛ teaspoon	¼ teaspoon
Poultry seasoning	½ teaspoon	1½ teaspoons

Heat butter in large skillet; add onion and celery and cook until transparent but not brown (about 10 minutes). Add bread cubes (¼- to ½-inch cubes) and seasonings. Heat until bread cubes are lightly browned and butter is absorbed, stirring constantly.

This recipe makes a somewhat dry and crumbly stuffing. For a stuffing that is more moist, add ⅓ to 1 cup chicken or turkey stock or water. Taste to correct seasonings.

Turkey Tetrazzini

8 ounces spaghetti, broken in pieces
5 tablespoons butter or margarine
6 tablespoons flour
3 cups chicken or turkey broth
1 cup light cream
1 teaspoon salt
Pepper
1 cup fresh or canned mushrooms, including juice
5 tablespoons minced green peppers
3 cups cooked turkey, cubed
½ cup grated Parmesan cheese
½ cup shredded Cheddar cheese

Cook spaghetti in boiling salted water until just tender (do not overcook). Melt butter; blend in flour. Stir broth into flour mixture. Add cream. Cook until mixture thickens and bubbles. Add salt and pepper, drained spaghetti, mushrooms, green peppers, and cooked turkey. Turn into individual baking dishes or into a 2- to 3-quart flat casserole. Sprinkle with cheeses. Bake at 350 degrees F. for about 30 minutes or until bubbly and lightly browned. Makes 8 servings.

Quick Chicken a la King

½ cup diced green pepper
½ tablespoon butter or margarine
1 can (10½ ounces) cream of mushroom or cream of chicken soup
1¼ cups milk
3 cups chicken, cooked and cubed
1 tablespoon pimiento, chopped
Dash of pepper

Cook green pepper in butter until tender. Add soup; stir to blend. Gradually add milk; gently stir in remaining ingredients. Heat until sauce is bubbling and flavors are blended. Serve in patty shells, on toast, rice, Chinese noodles, or biscuits. Makes 8 servings, ¾ cup each.

Chicken a la King

Ingredients	12 servings	24 servings	36 servings
Shortening	½ cup	1 cup	1½ cups
Mushrooms, sliced	1½ cups	3 cups	4½ cups
Onions, chopped	¾ tablespoon	1½ tablespoons	2¼ tablespoons
Flour	6 tablespoons	¾ cup	1 cup plus 2 tablespoons
Chicken soup stock or consommé *	3 cups	6 cups	9 cups
Milk	2 cups	1 quart	1½ quarts
Chicken, cooked, cubed	4 cups**	8 cups**	12 cups**
Green pepper, chopped	½ cup	1 cup	1½ cups
Pimientos, chopped	½ cup	1 cup	1½ cups
Lemon juice	2 tablespoons	4 tablespoons	5-6 tablespoons
*or use chicken soup base, dry mix plus	¼ cup	½ cup	¾ cup
water	3 cups	6 cups	9 cups

**1 pound cooked, cubed chicken equals about 3 cups.*

Melt shortening in large saucepan or dutch oven; add mushrooms and onions, and cook until lightly browned. Stir in flour and blend well. Gradually add stock and milk, stirring constantly. Cook until mixture thickens and comes to a boil. Fold in remaining ingredients. Serve on toast, rice, or in patty shells. Each serving is about ⅔ cup.

Apricot Chicken

2 tablespoons cornstarch
2 cups apricot nectar
1 envelope dry onion soup mix
2 frying chickens, cut up

Mix cornstarch in saucepan in a small amount of apricot nectar. Add remaining nectar and onion soup mix. Heat and stir until sauce thickens. Pour over chicken pieces that have been washed and dried and arranged in a 9x9-inch baking dish. Bake covered at 350 degrees F. for 45 minutes. Uncover and bake about 45 minutes or until chicken is tender. Baste several times with sauce. This sauce will coat chicken pieces for about 8 servings.

Triple Divan

2 packages (10 ounces each) frozen broccoli
  spears or 2 pounds fresh broccoli
¾ pound cooked ham (8 serving-size slices)
¾ pound sliced cooked turkey breast or 1 whole
  chicken breast, sliced
½ pound cooked shrimp
1 can (10½ ounces) cream of chicken soup
¾ cup mayonnaise
2 teaspoons curry powder
1 cup table cream*
1 cup evaporated milk*
3 tablespoons lemon juice
2 tablespoons butter or margarine
2 cups soft buttered crumbs
½ pound (2 cups) finely shredded sharp cheese

Cook broccoli according to package directions. Be careful not to overcook. Or trim stems from fresh broccoli, wash, then cook in boiling salted water until just tender crisp. Drain and arrange broccoli, in serving sizes, in a 2- to 3-quart shallow baking dish.

Arrange ham slices, then turkey slices, then shrimp over broccoli servings. Combine soup, mayonnaise, curry, cream, evaporated milk, and lemon juice. Heat and stir until mixture is smooth and warm. Pour sauce over meat combination. Melt butter in frying pan. Add bread crumbs and stir until all are buttery and slightly brown. Add the shredded cheese to the crumb mixture. Combine well, then spread over sauce in baking dish. Bake at 350 degrees F. until sauce is hot and bubbly and crumbs are crispy and golden, about ½ hour. Makes 8 servings.

2 cups whole milk may be used in place of table cream and evaporated milk.

Hawaiian Chicken

2 whole chicken breasts, halved
2 chicken legs with thighs
Flour
Salt
Cooking oil
Oil
1 can (15½ ounces) pineapple chunks
½ cup honey
2 tablespoons cornstarch
¾ cup cider vinegar
1 tablespoon soy sauce
¼ teaspoon ginger
1 chicken bouillon cube
1 green pepper, cut in ¼-inch strips

Roll chicken pieces in flour and sprinkle with salt. Brown in oil.

Drain pineapple; reserve pineapple chunks, and pour juice into measuring cup; add water to make 1½ cups. Add honey, cornstarch, vinegar, soy sauce, ginger, and bouillon cube; bring to a boil and boil 2 minutes, stirring constantly. Pour over chicken pieces in 2-quart baking dish.

Bake, uncovered, for 30 minutes. Add pineapple chunks and green pepper. Bake 30 minutes longer or until chicken is tender. Serve with cooked rice. Makes 4 to 6 servings.

Lion House Chicken Crepes

12 crepes (recipe below)
3 cups chicken broth or consommé
3 or 4 tablespoons cornstarch
3 cups cooked chicken pieces
1 cup grated Cheddar cheese

Make crepes. Make chicken glaze by heating chicken broth or consommé in saucepan. When hot, mix cornstarch with a little cold water and stir into broth until thickened. Mix about ½ cup chicken glaze with chicken pieces to moisten. Arrange chicken pieces in center of each crepe. Sprinkle with grated cheese. Fold over sides and place in baking pan. Heat in a 350-degree F. oven for 15 minutes or until heated through. To serve, place two crepes per serving on plate and spoon chicken glaze over top. Makes 6 servings.

Basic Crepe Recipe

3 eggs   **3 tablespoons butter, melted**
½ cup milk   **¾ cup all-purpose flour**
½ cup water   **½ teaspoon salt**

Combine all ingredients in blender container; blend about 1 minute. Scrape down sides with rubber spatula, and blend about 30 seconds more. Refrigerate batter for 1 hour. To cook, heat omelet, crepe, or regular frying pan on medium-high heat just hot enough to sizzle a drop of water. Brush lightly with melted butter. For each crepe, pour in just enough batter to cover bottom of pan, tipping and tilting pan to move batter quickly over bottom. If crepe has holes, add a drop or two of batter to patch. Cook until light brown on bottom and dry on top. Remove from pan and stack on plate. Makes 12 crepes.

Quick and Easy Quiche

6 to 8 slices bread
12 eggs, beaten
1 can (10 ounces) cream of mushroom soup
1 cup evaporated milk or light cream
¼ teaspoon nutmeg
1 teaspoon salt
Pinch of cayenne pepper
1 pound ham, diced
½ cup diced green onion
¼ cup diced green pepper
1 pound Swiss cheese, grated

In a greased 9x13-inch baking pan, place slices of bread tightly on the bottom of pan. Beat eggs; add soup, milk, and seasonings. Sprinkle diced ham, onion, and green pepper over bread. Cover with egg and milk mixture. Sprinkle cheese over top. Cover with aluminum foil. Bake in 325-degree F. oven for 45 minutes. Remove foil and bake another 15 minutes uncovered. Cut into squares and serve. Makes 15 servings.

Variations: In place of ham, used cooked and crumbled bacon, cooked sausage, crab, or shrimp.

Cornish Game Hens

6 whole Rock Island Cornish Game Hens
3 cups Bread Stuffing (page 42)
2 cups chicken broth (use canned chicken consommé or chicken bouillon cubes dissolved in water)
3 tablespoons cornstarch
Salt and pepper

To thaw game hens, leave in original wrappers and thaw in refrigerator for 24 hours or immerse in cool water for 2 to 3 hours. When thawed, wash inside with cold water. Stuff with dressing, using ½ cup per bird. Place breast side up in a shallow baking pan; brush with butter or oil. Roast uncovered in a 350-degree F. oven for 1 hour and 15 minutes, basting with oil or butter several times during baking.

Prepare chicken glaze: Heat chicken broth or consommé in a saucepan. Mix cornstarch with a small amount of cold water, and stir into hot broth until thickened. Season with salt and pepper.

To serve, pour chicken glaze over baked game hens. Makes 6 servings.

Fish and Shellfish

Broiled Fish Steaks or Fillets

8 fish steaks or fillets, washed well in cold
   running water
Salt
Paprika
¼ cup lemon juice
½ cup melted butter or margarine
¼ cup chopped parsley

Place fillets or steaks on well-greased baking sheet. Sprinkle with salt and paprika. Drip lemon juice and butter generously over fish. Broil about 6 inches from heat for approximately 10 minutes for each 1 inch of thickness, basting once with lemon and butter. When fish is firm and flakes easily, remove from broiler. Baste again with lemon and butter; garnish with parsley and serve immediately. Makes 8 servings.

Lemon Fish Bake

8 fish fillets, large enough for 1 serving each,
   washed well in cold running water
Salt
5 tablespoons butter or margarine (about)
1 lemon, thinly sliced
¼ to ½ cup sour cream
½ cup Cheddar cheese, shredded
Lemon Sauce (below)

Place fillets in a single layer in a shallow buttered baking dish. Salt each fillet lightly, then top with about 2 teaspoons of melted butter. Cover baking dish with foil. Place in 450-degree F. oven and bake until fish flakes easily with a fork. Don't overcook, or fish

will be dry. Allow about 10 minutes for each inch of thickness.

When fish is baked, drain off part of liquid and cover with Lemon Sauce. Serve each fillet topped with a thin slice of lemon, a dollop of sour cream, and shredded cheese. Makes 8 servings.

Lemon Sauce

1 tablespoon cornstarch
1 tablespoon butter or margarine
1½ cups water
¼ cup lemon juice

Make a paste of cornstarch and butter. Bring water and lemon juice to a boil. Stir in cornstarch paste and cook until thickened. Use about 2 tablespoons sauce on each fillet.

Creamy Baked Halibut Steaks

4 halibut steaks, about ¾-inch thick
Salt
Pepper
¾ cup thick sour cream
¼ cup dry bread crumbs
¼ teaspoon garlic salt
1½ teaspoons chopped chives, fresh or frozen
⅓ cup grated Parmesan cheese
1 teaspoon paprika

Place steaks, close fitting, in a shallow buttered baking dish. Sprinkle with salt and pepper. Mix together sour cream, bread crumbs, garlic salt, and chives, and spread over steaks. Sprinkle with Parmesan cheese and paprika. Bake, uncovered, at 400 degrees F. for 15 to 20 minutes, or until fish flakes with a fork. Makes 4 large or 8 small servings.

Halibut au Gratin

1 to 1½ pounds halibut
2 to 3 tablespoons each chopped onion,
    celery, carrot
¼ teaspoon salt
6 tablespoons butter or margarine
6 tablespoons flour
½ teaspoon salt
⅛ teaspoon white pepper
2½ cups milk
½ cup grated Parmesan cheese
2 cups shredded sharp Cheddar cheese
¼ cup chopped pimiento

In a large frying pan, place halibut pieces in a single layer; spread chopped onion, celery, and carrot over them. Add ¼ teaspoon salt to small amount of water (about ½ cup) and pour into pan with fish. Cover and steam gently until fish flakes easily with a fork (about 20 minutes). Turn the fish after about 10 minutes. Remove fish from pan, scrape off vegetables that cling to it, and when cool enough to handle, remove skin and bones; break fish into large chunks.

In the meantime, make a white sauce: melt butter in a small saucepan. Add flour, salt, and pepper, and stir over medium heat until the mixture foams. Add milk, and stir occasionally until sauce is thick and smooth. Pour half of sauce in a 2-quart casserole or a 9x9-inch shallow baking dish. Layer fish chunks over sauce, then Parmesan cheese, then Cheddar cheese. Cover with remaining white sauce. Sprinkle with chopped pimiento. Bake at 350 degrees F. for about 30 minutes or until hot and bubbly. Do not overcook or fish will be tough and dry. Makes 6 servings.

Baked Salmon Steaks

6 salmon steaks, cut about ¾ inch thick, washed
    well in cold running water
⅓ cup melted butter
3 tablespoons fresh lemon juice (or more to
    taste)
½ teaspoon salt

Arrange salmon steaks in a shallow, greased baking pan, in a single layer. Combine butter, lemon juice, and salt, and spoon over the steaks. Bake uncovered in a 350-degree F. oven for 15 to 20 minutes, or until fish flakes easily with a fork. Remove salmon to a warm serving platter; keep warm.

Pour pan drippings into a warm serving dish. Add more lemon juice if desired. Pass to spoon over salmon. Makes 6 servings.

Salmon Roll

⅓ cup diced onions
⅓ cup diced celery
⅓ cup diced green peppers
2 tablespoons butter or margarine
1 can (about 7 ounces) salmon, skin removed
½ cup cream of mushroom soup (taken from
    10½-ounce can)
¼ cup stuffed olives, sliced
⅔ cup water (about)
2 cups biscuit mix
Melted butter or margarine

Sauté onions, celery, and peppers in butter. Drain and flake salmon; reserve liquid. Combine sautéed mixture with salmon, soup, and olives.

Add water to biscuit mix and stir together to make soft dough. Gently smooth dough into a ball on a floured board. Knead 5 times, then roll ¼-inch thick into a rectangle. Cover with salmon mixture to within 1 inch of edges. Roll up, jelly-roll style, starting with short end. Seal edges and ends well. Place roll on a greased shallow baking pan, sealed ↗

side down. Brush with melted butter. Bake at 350 degrees F. for 50 to 60 minutes. Makes 6 servings.

Sauce

Mushroom soup left from Salmon Roll filling
2 tablespoons lemon juice
⅓ cup salmon liquid (drained from salmon)
½ cup milk

Combine ingredients and heat. Serve over Salmon Roll.

Salmon Tetrazzini

1 can (15½ ounces) salmon, skin removed
½ pound mushrooms, sliced
2 cloves garlic, minced
½ cup chopped green onions
¼ cup butter or margarine
¼ cup flour
1 cup chicken broth
1½ cups half-and-half cream
2 tablespoons lemon juice
½ teaspoon salt
⅛ teaspoon pepper
¼ cup grated Parmesan cheese
8 ounces spaghetti, cooked
3 tablespoons grated Parmesan cheese
Lemon slice and parsley for garnish (if desired)

Drain and flake salmon, reserving liquid. Sauté mushrooms, garlic, and green onions in butter or margarine. Blend in flour. Gradually add chicken broth, half-and-half, lemon juice, and reserved salmon liquid. Cook, stirring constantly, until thickened and smooth. Add seasonings, ¼ cup grated Parmesan cheese, and salmon. Combine with spaghetti. Taste to correct seasonings.

Turn into buttered 2½-quart casserole. Sprinkle with 3 tablespoons grated Parmesan cheese. Bake at 375 degrees F. for 20 to 25 minutes, until bubbly and slightly browned. Garnish with slice of lemon and sprig of parsley. Makes 6 to 8 servings.

Note: Salmon Tetrazzini may be prepared in advance and refrigerated or frozen.

Salmon Mousse

2 envelopes (2 tablespoons) unflavored gelatin
½ cup cold water
1 cup boiling water
3 tablespoons lemon juice
2 cups flaked, cold, cooked salmon*
½ cup mayonnaise
2 tablespoons capers (or use chopped sweet pickles)
1 tablespoon minced onion
1 tablespoon Worcestershire sauce
1 teaspoon salt*
½ teaspoon Tabasco sauce
½ cup heavy cream
Cucumber Sauce or Dill-Sour Cream Sauce

Add gelatin to cold water; let stand about 5 minutes. Add boiling water and stir until gelatin is dissolved. Add lemon juice. Cool.

Mix salmon with mayonnaise, capers, onion, Worcestershire sauce, salt, and Tabasco sauce. Add to gelatin mixture and beat until smooth. Chill until slightly thickened.

Whip cream. Fold into salmon mixture. Pour into 4- or 5-cup mold. Chill until firm, at least 2 hours. Unmold and serve with Cucumber Sauce or Dill-Sour Cream Sauce. Makes about 4½ cups, or 6 servings.

Note: Mousse may be made a day ahead and stored, covered, in refrigerator.

Or use 1 can (1 pound) salmon; discard bones and skin and reduce salt to ½ teaspoon.

Dill-Sour Cream Sauce

1 cup sour cream
1 tablespoon fresh dill weed or 1 teaspoon dried dill weed
2 teaspoons lemon juice
½ teaspoon sugar
½ teaspoon salt

Combine all ingredients and blend well. Serve chilled with Salmon Mousse. Makes about 1 cup.

Cucumber Sauce

2 cucumbers, peeled and chopped
½ cup sour cream
½ cup mayonnaise
2 tablespoons chopped chives
¼ teaspoon dry mustard
¼ teaspoon salt

Combine all ingredients and blend well. Serve chilled with Salmon Mousse. Makes about 1⅔ cups.

Shrimp Creole with Rice

2½ tablespoons butter or margarine
½ cup chopped green pepper
⅓ cup chopped green onions (use some of the green tops)
1 cup chopped celery
2 tablespoons flour
⅛ teaspoon paprika
1 can (1 pound 12 ounces) whole tomatoes, drained (reserve liquid)
2 cups reserved tomato liquid, heated
1 small bay leaf
2 cans (about 5 ounces each) shrimp, drained (or use 1½ pounds fresh shrimp, cooked)
1 tablespoon chopped parsley (or use ¾ teaspoon dry parsley flakes)
Salt to taste
Cooked rice

Melt butter in large frying pan or dutch oven. Sauté green pepper, onions, and celery until soft but not brown (5 to 10 minutes on low heat.) Add flour and paprika; blend well. Add hot tomato liquid; cook and stir until smooth and thick. Add whole tomatoes and bay leaf. Cover and simmer 30 minutes. Add shrimp and continue cooking until shrimp is heated (about 5 minutes). Add parsley. Taste to correct seasonings. Serve immediately over hot cooked rice. Makes 6 servings.

Seafood Newburg

¼ cup minced onion
¼ cup minced green pepper (optional)
1 cup butter
1 cup flour
¼ cup chopped pimiento (optional)
1 tablespoon paprika
1 teaspoon salt
¼ teaspoon white pepper
Dash cayenne
4 cups milk, heated
1 cup light cream (about)
2 tablespoons lemon juice (about)
4 cups cooked seafood and fish*
Pastry shells, cooked rice, or crisp toast

Make a thick white sauce: In the top of a 3- or 4-quart double boiler placed over medium heat, sauté onion and green pepper in butter, covered, until soft but not brown (about 5 minutes). Blend in flour and seasonings. Add hot milk and stir until mixture is very thick. Add part of cream, to desired consistency. Place pan over boiling water. Cover and cook for about 10 minutes.

Add lemon juice, seafood, and fish. Add more cream if necessary. Taste to correct seasonings. Serve in pastry shells or over hot cooked rice or buttered toast. Makes about 2 quarts, or about 10 servings.

Note: The Newburg sauce may be prepared and frozen up to a month in advance. Thaw overnight in refrigerator and reheat over boiling water, stirring frequently. If necessary, blend with a whip or rotary beater until smooth. Then add seafood and lemon juice. Taste to correct seasonings.

Use at least 2 cups shrimp, crabmeat, lobster or scallops. The remainder may be flaked cooked white fish, such as cod, haddock, halibut or sole.

Shrimp-Cheese Fondue

3 cans (4½ ounces) shrimp,* deveined
3 cups broken pieces white bread
2 cups grated sharp Cheddar cheese
9 eggs, lightly beaten
4½ cups milk
1½ teaspoons salt
¾ teaspoon dry mustard
3 teaspoons minced onion
¼ teaspoon pepper

Layer shrimp, bread, and cheese in a greased 2-quart casserole. Combine the remaining ingredients and pour over layered shrimp in casserole. Bake at 350 degrees F. for about one hour, or until set. Makes 12 servings.

Canned crab meat may be used in place of shrimp.

Tuna Chow Mein Casserole

1 tablespoon butter or margarine
1 cup chopped celery
¼ cup chopped onion
2 tablespoons chopped green pepper
½ can (5½-ounce) chow mein noodles
1 can (about 7 ounces) tuna, with liquid
1 can (10½ ounces) cream of mushroom soup
¼ cup milk
¼ cup water
⅛ teaspoon pepper

Melt butter in large skillet. Add celery, onion, and green pepper; cook and stir until onion is tender. Reserving ¼ cup chow mein noodles, stir in remaining ingredients. Pour mixture into ungreased 1½-quart casserole; sprinkle reserved chow mein noodles over top. Bake at 350 degrees F., uncovered, for 30 minutes. Makes 4 to 6 servings.

Hot Stuffed Avocado

4 large avocados, peeled and halved lengthwise
¼ cup lemon juice
Pinch garlic powder
¼ cup butter or margarine
2 tablespoons chopped green onion
½ teaspoon celery salt
Dash cayenne pepper
¼ cup flour
2 cups light cream
1 to 2 cups cooked crabmeat, shrimp, chicken, or turkey
1 cup sharp Cheddar cheese, grated

Roll outside of peeled avocados in lemon juice to keep color. Cut avocados in half; remove pits, and place avocados in large baking pan. Sprinkle with lemon juice and garlic powder. Meanwhile, melt butter; add green onion, celery salt, and cayenne pepper; cook 5 minutes. Blend in flour. Add cream, and cook, stirring until thickened. Fold in the seafood or poultry and ½ cup cheese. Taste to correct seasonings.

Place avocados in a 350-degree F. oven and bake for 15 minutes. Remove from oven and arrange on serving plates. Ladle filling over avocados. Top with remaining cheese. Serve immediately. Makes 8 servings.

Tartar Sauce

1 cup mayonnaise
1 cup salad dressing
1 tablespoon sweet pickle relish
1 tablespoon minced raw onion
½ tablespoon lemon juice
1 drop Tabasco sauce

Mix all ingredients together until well blended. Serve with fish. Makes 2 cups sauce.

Vegetables

German Green Beans

1 cup water
1 tablespoon vinegar
1 medium onion, finely chopped
2 pounds green beans, cleaned and cut into
    ½-inch pieces
½ teaspoon salt
2 tablespoons bacon drippings

In saucepan combine water, vinegar, and onion. Bring to boil; add beans. Cover; simmer for about 20 minutes or until beans are tender. Add salt and bacon drippings. Cook, uncovered, over high heat for 5 minutes. Makes 6 to 8 servings.

Note: Canned green beans may be used. Use two 1-pound cans, drained. Use 1 cup liquid drained from beans in place of water.

South of the Border Beans

6 slices of bacon
½ cup finely chopped onion
½ cup chopped celery
3 cups cooked green beans
1 can (8 ounces) tomato sauce
1 teaspoon Worcestershire sauce
Salt and pepper to taste
½ cup bread crumbs, buttered

Sauté the bacon, onion, and celery together. Combine the beans, tomato sauce, Worcestershire sauce, salt and pepper, and bacon mixture. Turn into greased 1½-quart casserole, and top with buttered crumbs. Bake uncovered in 375-degree F. oven for 20 minutes. Makes 6 servings.

Green Beans Parisienne

2 cans (1 pound each) cut green beans, or 2
    packages (10 ounces each) frozen or
    1 pound fresh green beans, cooked
1 can (10½ ounces) cream of mushroom soup
½ cup water or milk
½ teaspoon Worcestershire sauce, or use 1
    teaspoon soy sauce
½ cup shredded Cheddar cheese

Cook frozen or fresh beans, or drain canned beans. Drain well. Stir soup to a smooth sauce with water and Worcestershire sauce. Combine soup mixture with green beans and pour into a 2-quart baking dish. Top with shredded cheese. Bake at 350 degrees F. for 30 minutes, or until cheese melts and browns slightly. Makes 4 to 6 servings.

Lemon Carrots and Apples

12 medium-sized carrots, cut in thin slices
½ teaspoon salt
1 teaspoon grated lemon peel
¼ cup butter or margarine
2 large tart apples, peeled, cored, and cut in
    ⅓-inch-thick slices
2 tablespoons chopped parsley

Put carrots in a shallow 2-quart casserole. Sprinkle with salt and lemon peel and dot with butter. Bake, covered, in a 375-degree F. oven until almost tender, about 30 minutes. Stir in apples, cover, and bake 10 to 20 minutes more, or until apples are tender. Stir well just before serving, and sprinkle with parsley. Makes about 8 servings.

Glazed Broccoli with Almonds

2 pounds broccoli or 2 packages (10 ounces)
   frozen broccoli
½ teaspoon salt
1 chicken bouillon cube
¾ cup hot water
¼ cup butter or margarine
¼ cup flour
1 cup light cream
2 tablespoons lemon juice
½ teaspoon monosodium glutamate (MSG)
Pepper to taste
¼ cup grated Parmesan cheese
¼ cup slivered blanched almonds

Preheat oven to 375 degrees F. Grease a 9x9-inch baking pan. Separate broccoli; trim stems and wash thoroughly. Add salt, and cook in boiling water for 12 minutes or until barely tender. Drain and arrange in baking pan.

While broccoli is cooking, prepare sauce. Dissolve bouillon cube in ¾ cup hot water. Melt butter or margarine in saucepan; blend in flour. Gradually stir in cream and dissolved bouillon cube; cook over medium heat, stirring constantly, until thickened and smooth. Remove from heat and stir in lemon juice, monosodium glutamate, salt, and pepper. Taste to correct seasoning. Pour sauce over broccoli. Sprinkle with cheese and almonds. Bake for 20 minutes or until golden brown. Makes 6 to 8 servings.

Sesame Green Beans

Wash 1 pound fresh green beans. Snip ends and cut into ¼- to ½-inch lengths. Cook in boiling salted water until just tender. Drain. Serve with hot Sesame-Soy Sauce. Makes 4 servings.

Sesame-Soy Sauce

1 tablespoon toasted sesame seeds
1 tablespoon soy sauce
2 tablespoons butter or margarine, melted

Combine ingredients and heat. Serve over green beans. Sauce is also good on cooked, well-drained spinach or asparagus.

Savory Cabbage

1 medium head cabbage, shredded
½ teaspoon salt
Water
2 tablespoons butter or margarine
1 teaspoon finely chopped green onion
¼ cup cream
Pepper

Cook cabbage in salted boiling water to cover until just tender. Drain well. In large skillet, melt butter; add onion, and cook for about 5 minutes, or until onion is soft but not brown. Add cabbage and mix well. Pour the cream over the cabbage, and sprinkle with pepper. Serve at once. Makes 4 to 6 servings.

Almond Celery Casserole

4 cups celery, sliced on the diagonal
1 can (10 ounces) cream of celery soup
½ cup sour cream
1 cup water chestnuts, sliced
½ cup shredded sharp Cheddar cheese
½ cup slivered almonds
½ cup seasoned bread crumbs (stuffing
   mix)

Cook celery in lightly salted boiling water, just until tender-crisp. Drain well and add sour cream and water chestnuts. Pour into a shallow 2-quart baking dish. Top with cheese, then almonds, then bread crumbs. Bake in a 350-degree F. oven for 30 minutes, or until hot and lightly browned. Makes 4 to 6 servings.

Beets and Onions

2 tablespoons butter or margarine
2 cups sliced pickled beets, drained
1 cup sliced thin onion rings
2 teaspoons sugar
½ teaspoon salt
Pepper

Melt the butter and add beets and onion rings. Simmer covered for 15 minutes. Add seasonings. Makes 4 servings.

Stewed Cabbage and Carrots

2 cups shredded carrots
1 cup boiling water
3 cups shredded cabbage
2 tablespoons butter or margarine
1 teaspoon salt

Cook carrots in boiling water until partly tender, about 5 minutes. Add cabbage and simmer, uncovered, for 10 minutes. Add butter and salt and cook five minutes. Most of the liquid should be absorbed in the cooking and the vegetables served without draining. Makes 6 servings.

Caraway Cabbage

½ cup chopped onion
2 tablespoons butter or margarine, melted
1 cup water
2 teaspoons sugar
1 teaspoon salt
1¼ teaspoon caraway seed
2 teaspoons white vinegar
½ large head red cabbage

In large saucepan over medium heat, cook onion in hot butter until tender. Add water and remaining ingredients. Simmer, covered, 8 minutes or until cabbage is tender-crisp. Serve immediately. Makes about 6 servings.

Broccoli with Mustard Sauce

3 pounds fresh broccoli, cleaned and heavy part of stems removed (3 packages of frozen broccoli may be used, cooked as directed on package)
2 tablespoons finely chopped onion
3 tablespoons butter or margarine
3 tablespoons flour
1½ cups milk (or use part chicken stock)
3 tablespoons lemon juice
2 tablespoons prepared mustard
2 teaspoons sugar
1 teaspoon salt

Cook broccoli in boiling salted water until just tender-crisp. While broccoli cooks, sauté the onion in butter until tender but not brown (about 5 minutes). Stir in the flour, then gradually add the milk; stir and cook until smooth and thickened. Add remaining ingredients. Serve on well-drained hot broccoli. Makes 8 servings.

Italian Green Beans

4 slices thick bacon
2 tablespoons bacon drippings
1 green onion, chopped
1 tablespoon chopped green pepper
1 can (16 ounces) green beans, drained
1 can (16 ounces) seasoned tomatoes
½ teaspoon salt

Sauté bacon in hot frying pan until cooked but not crisp. Remove from pan. Measure 2 tablespoons of drippings back into the frying pan. Add onion and green pepper and cook until soft but not brown, about 5 minutes. Add green beans, seasoned tomatoes, salt, and bacon pieces. Stir; cover, and simmer for 20 minutes. Makes 6 servings.

Baked Beans

2 cans (29 ounces each) pork and beans
2 large onions, chopped
2 large green peppers, chopped
1 cup catsup
1 cup brown sugar
2 teaspoons Worcestershire sauce
1 pound lean bacon, cut up and cooked
    crisp, then drained

Combine ingredients well in a 9x13-inch baking pan. Bake 2½ hours, covered with aluminum foil, at 325 degrees F. Uncover and bake another 30 minutes. Makes 8 to 10 servings.

Pineapple Carrots

3 cups sliced carrots
1 cup pineapple chunks, unsweetened,
    canned or fresh
½ teaspoon seasoned salt
3 tablespoons orange juice
1 tablespoon butter or margarine

Place carrots, pineapple, salt, and orange juice in 1½-quart casserole. Dot with butter. Cover. Bake in 375-degree F. oven for 45 to 55 minutes. Makes 4 servings.

Harvard Beets

3 cups sliced cooked beets, drained
½ cup vinegar
½ cup water and drained beet liquid
1 tablespoon cornstarch
1 teaspoon sugar
Dash ground cloves
Dash salt
1 tablespoon butter

Heat together vinegar, water and beet juice, cornstarch, sugar, cloves, and salt. Stir until thickened. Add beets and butter and reheat. Makes 6 to 8 servings.

Company Cauliflower

2 teaspoons sesame seeds
1 medium head cauliflower
Dash salt
Dash pepper
1 cup sour cream
½ to 1 cup shredded Cheddar cheese

In shallow pan toast sesame seeds on medium heat for 10 minutes or until browned, shaking pan occasionally. Rinse cauliflower and separate into small flowerets. Cook in a 2-quart covered saucepan, in 1 inch boiling salted water, 8 to 10 minutes, or until tender; drain well. Place half of cauliflower in 1-quart casserole. Season with salt and pepper; spread over ½ cup sour cream and sprinkle with half of cheese; top with 1 teaspoon sesame seeds. Repeat. Bake in a 375-degree F. oven 15 minutes, or until heated through. Makes 6 servings.

Potato Casserole

5 large potatoes
3 tablespoons butter or margarine, melted
1 can (10½ ounces) cream of chicken
    soup
1 cup sour cream
1 cup milk
3 tablespoons finely chopped green onions
¾ cup shredded sharp Cheddar cheese
¾ cup cornflake crumbs (or dry bread
    crumbs), mixed with melted butter
2 tablespoons butter or margarine, melted
3 tablespoons Parmesan cheese

Boil unpared potatoes until tender. Drain and peel. Shred coarsely. Place in 2- or 3-quart casserole. Pour melted butter over potatoes. Mix together soup, sour cream, milk, onions, and cheese. Pour evenly over potatoes. Do not mix. Cover the top with buttered crumbs mixed with Parmesan cheese. Bake 30 minutes at 325 degrees F. Makes 8 to 10 servings.

Crumb-Topped Baked Onions

18 to 20 small white boiling onions
1 chicken bouillon cube
¾ cup water
2 tablespoons melted butter or margarine
½ teaspoon sage
¼ teaspoon pepper
1½ teaspoons cornstarch blended with 1
    tablespoon water
¼ cup croutons, slightly crushed
2 tablespoons grated Parmesan cheese
1 tablespoon chopped parsley

Peel onions and arrange in a single layer in an 8- or 9-inch baking dish. Crush bouillon cube, then stir in the water and heat until dissolved. Stir in the melted butter, sage, and pepper. Pour over onions. Cover and bake in a 350-degree F. oven for about 1 hour or until tender when pierced. Transfer onions to a heated serving dish; keep warm.

Pour cooking juices into a small saucepan. Stir in the cornstarch mixture and cook, stirring, until sauce boils and thickens. Pour over onions. Combine the croutons, Parmesan cheese, and chopped parsley; sprinkle evenly over onions. Makes 4 to 6 servings.

Rice Pilaf

2 tablespoons butter or margarine
1 cup uncooked rice
¼ cup minced onion
⅓ cup minced celery
3 cups hot chicken broth
2 tablespoons chopped parsley
¼ cup slivered almonds

Melt butter in hot frying pan. Add rice, onion, and celery; stir and cook until slightly brown. Add chicken broth. Cover and simmer on low heat until moisture has been absorbed and rice is tender. Add parsley and almonds just before serving. Toss lightly. Makes 8 ½-cup servings.

Creamed Onions

2 to 3 pounds small white onions, peeled
    (18 to 24 onions)
4 tablespoons butter or margarine
4 tablespoons flour
1 teaspoon salt
⅛ teaspoon pepper
2 cups milk

Cook onions in boiling salted water in a medium saucepan for about 20 minutes or until tender (be careful not to overcook). Drain; return to saucepan. While onions cook, melt butter over low heat in a small saucepan; blend in flour, salt, and pepper; stir until bubbly. Stir in milk; continue cooking and stirring until sauce thickens and boils 1 minute. Pour over drained onions; heat slowly until bubbly. Makes 6 to 8 servings.

Pineappled Sweet Potatoes

6 medium sweet potatoes or yams, cooked
    and peeled
⅓ cup sugar
⅓ cup brown sugar
¼ teaspoon salt
2 tablespoons cornstarch
½ cup pineapple juice
½ cup orange juice
1 can (13¼ ounces) pineapple chunks, well
    drained (or use pineapple tidbits or
    crushed pineapple)
2 tablespoons butter or margarine

Cook sweet potatoes in boiling salted water until tender. Cut into thick slices; arrange in shallow baking dish. Stir and blend well the sugars, salt, and cornstarch in a heavy saucepan. In a small saucepan, bring fruit juices to a boil; gradually add to sugar mixture. Cook and stir until thickened. Add pineapple and butter. Pour over potatoes. Serve immediately, or place in a 350-degree F. oven just until bubbly hot. Makes 8 servings.

Honeyed Onions

Small, raw, whole peeled onions (about 16)
1 can (8 ounces) tomato sauce
½ cup honey
⅓ cup butter or margarine

Simmer onions in tomato sauce, honey, and butter. Cook slowly until tender. Let stand in syrup. Reheat (the more times the better) and serve. If syrup boils down, add a little water or tomato juice. Makes 4 servings.

Green Beans Parmesan

Size of serving: approximately ½ cup

Ingredients	12 servings	25 servings
Bacon, diced	6 ounces	12 ounces
Onions, finely chopped	¾ cup	1½ cups
Green beans, canned, cut	6 cups	1 No. 10 can
Salt*	¼ teaspoon	¾ teaspoon
Cornflake crumbs	½ cup	1 cup (3 oz.)
Parmesan cheese, grated	½ cup	1 cup (4 oz.)

*Amount of salt will depend on "saltiness" of beans.

Fry bacon until crisp; remove from fat and drain. Cook onions in bacon fat until tender, stirring constantly. Drain off most of bacon fat. Heat green beans; drain well. Add bacon, onions, salt, cornflake crumbs, and cheese to green beans; toss lightly until thoroughly mixed. Serve immediately.

Hungarian Green Beans

1½ pounds green beans
1½ cups boiling water
½ teaspoon salt
6 slices bacon, chopped
1 onion, finely chopped
2 tablespoons flour
1 tablespoon vinegar
⅔ cup sour cream

Trim ends of beans; break into 1-inch lengths. Put in saucepan with water and salt. Bring to boil; cover; simmer for about 25 minutes.

Meanwhile, cook bacon in skillet until crisp. Add onion; sauté until transparent. Stir in flour. Stir in vinegar. Gradually stir in hot liquid from beans; cook, stirring, until creamy and smooth. Add beans. Stir in sour cream. Cover and let stand for 2 minutes before serving. Makes 6 servings.

Potatoes in Sour Cream

2 pounds potatoes (about 6 medium)
2 tablespoons butter or margarine
1 medium onion, minced
¼ cup bread crumbs
¼ cup shredded sharp Cheddar cheese
2 eggs, slightly beaten
1 cup sour cream
½ teaspoon salt
⅛ teaspoon pepper

Scrub potatoes and cook in boiling salted water. Drain, then peel and slice into a 2-quart baking dish. Melt butter in a skillet; add onions and brown slightly. Add onions, bread crumbs, and cheese to potatoes. Beat eggs and stir into sour cream. Add salt and pepper. Pour over potatoes. Bake at 350 degrees F. for 15 to 20 minutes, until well-heated and slightly brown. Makes 6 servings.

Potatoes Au Gratin

12 medium-sized potatoes, cooked
6 tablespoons butter or margarine
6 tablespoons flour
3 teaspoons salt
Pepper
4 cups milk, heated
2 cups shredded cheese

Dice cooked potatoes. Melt the butter in a saucepan and stir in the flour and seasonings. Cook, stirring constantly, until the mixture bubbles. Gradually add the milk, and cook over low heat, stirring constantly until the sauce boils and thickens. Stir in ¾ cup grated cheese and the diced potatoes. Turn into a baking dish, top with the rest of the cheese, and bake at 375 degrees F. about 15 minutes, until the cheese melts and browns. Makes about 14 to 16 servings.

Baked Summer Squash

4 medium-size yellow crookneck squash
Salt
1 small onion, finely chopped
2 tablespoons butter or margarine
½ cup cream
¼ cup saltine crackers, crushed
Butter and soft bread crumbs

Slice squash and boil in salted water until tender. Drain well and mash. Sauté onion in butter until transparent but not brown (5 to 10 minutes). Add to squash. Add cream and cracker crumbs. Pour into a greased one-quart casserole. Dot with butter and a few soft bread crumbs. Bake at 400 degrees F. for about ½ hour, or until firm. Makes 4 to 6 servings.

Vegetable Medley

2 medium carrots
3 small zucchini
3 ribs of celery
Water
2 tablespoons butter
Salt and pepper to taste

Peel carrots; wash and clean zucchini and celery. Slice vegetables on the diagonal to make "off balance" rounds. Bring to a boil ¼ inch water and butter. Add the carrots and simmer, covered, for 4 minutes. Add the celery and simmer an additional 2 minutes. Add the zucchini and continue cooking for an additional 5 minutes, or until all vegetables are tender-crisp. Season to taste with salt and pepper. Serve at once, retaining the remaining liquid in the serving dish. Makes 4 servings.

Vegetable Medley No. 2: Combine cooked, sliced small yellow summer squash with a package of cooked green peas. Season with salt, pepper, and butter.

Vegetable Medley No. 3: Combine sliced zucchini with sliced yellow summer squash. Season with salt, pepper, and butter.

Chinese Spinach

1 pound fresh spinach
2 tablespoons salad oil
2 tablespoons soy sauce
½ teaspoon sugar
2 tablespoons finely chopped onion
1 8-ounce can water chestnuts, drained and
   sliced

Wash and pat spinach leaves dry. Tear into bite-size pieces. In large saucepan, simmer spinach with a small amount of water for 3 minutes; drain thoroughly. Heat oil, soy sauce, and sugar in skillet; add spinach and onion. Cook and toss until spinach is well-coated, 2 to 3 minutes. Stir in water chestnuts. Makes 4 servings.

Zucchini with Ground Beef

8 medium zucchini
1 pound lean ground beef
1 medium onion
1 clove garlic
2 tablespoons chopped green pepper
1 tablespoon salad oil
Pinch salt, rosemary, thyme, marjoram, pepper
½ cup Parmesan cheese
⅔ cup cracker crumbs
1 can (8 ounces) tomato sauce
½ cup water
1 bouillon cube

Wash zucchini; boil in salted water 10 minutes. Cut lengthwise in halves and scoop out insides. Drain scooped-out portion and mash well. Sauté beef, onion, garlic, and green pepper in oil for 5 minutes. Stir with fork; add zucchini pulp, salt, herbs, all but 2 tablespoons cheese, and all but 2 tablespoons crumbs. Heap mixture into zucchini shells. Place in shallow baking dish. Heat tomato sauce, water, and bouillon cube until cube is dissolved. Pour over zucchini. Sprinkle with remaining cheese and crumbs. Bake 45 minutes at 350 degrees F., basting once or twice. Makes 8 servings, 2 stuffed shells each.

Stuffed Zucchini No. 1

3 medium zucchini
1 package (10 ounces) frozen spinach, cooked
2 tablespoons flour
½ cup milk
Salt
⅓ cup shredded Cheddar cheese
3 strips bacon, cut in half

Trim off ends of zucchini; cook, drain, and cut in half lengthwise. Scoop out pulp; drain and chop the pulp and add to cooked spinach.

Blend flour and milk; cook and stir until thick. Add spinach-zucchini mixture. Salt cavity of zucchini shell. Put creamed filling in, and top with cheese and bacon. Bake 20 minutes at 350 degrees F. Makes 6 servings, ½ zucchini each.

Yam and Apple Casserole

6 medium yams
3 or 4 apples, peeled, cored, and sliced
½ cup butter or margarine
3 tablespoons cornstarch
1 cup sugar
1 teaspoon salt
2 cups water
2 tablespoons lemon juice

Parboil yams about 20 minutes. Cool, peel, and slice in layers in a buttered casserole, alternating yam slices with apple slices. Melt butter in small saucepan. Add cornstarch, sugar, and salt and blend well. Add water; cook and stir until sauce thickens. Add lemon juice, then pour sauce over yams and apples. Bake at 350 degrees F. for one hour. Makes 8 servings.

Green Bean Casserole

1½ pounds ground beef
¾ cup chopped onions
¾ teaspoon oregano
¼ teaspoon basil or thyme
½ teaspoon salt
¼ teaspoon pepper
1 can (10½ ounces) tomato soup
1 cup tomato juice
1 can (16 ounces) cut green beans, drained
2 or 3 cups mashed potatoes (use packaged instant potatoes, if desired)

Brown meat in a heavy frying pan. Drain off excess fat. Add onions and cook until tender. Stir in seasonings. Add tomato soup, tomato juice, and drained green beans. Mix until well blended and simmer for a few minutes to blend flavors. Pour into a 2-quart casserole dish and spoon mounds of hot mashed potatoes on top. Dot with butter. Bake for 20 to 30 minutes in a 375-degree F. oven.

Cheese Sauce

3 tablespoons butter or margarine
3 tablespoons flour
1½ teaspoons prepared mustard
1½ cups milk
½ pound grated Cheddar cheese
½ teaspoon salt
1 dash hot pepper sauce
1 tablespoon onion juice
1 tablespoon Worcestershire sauce

Melt butter; add flour and mustard, and blend together. Add milk; stir over medium heat until thick. Stir in cheese, salt, hot pepper sauce, onion juice, and Worcestershire sauce. Stir until thick. Remove from heat. Serve on cauliflower, broccoli, or cabbage. Enough for 8 to 10 servings.

Stuffed Zucchini No. 2

4 zucchini (about 2 pounds)
2 tablespoons butter or margarine
2 green onions, chopped
½ pound fresh mushrooms, cleaned and chopped
½ cup chopped walnuts
1 cup fresh bread crumbs
4 eggs
2 tablespoons chopped parsley
1 tablespoon chopped basil
Salt and pepper to taste
½ cup grated Cheddar or Parmesan cheese

Scrub zucchini and cut in half lengthwise. Scoop out and reserve pulp, leaving shells ¼-inch thick. Parboil shells 5 minutes. Chop pulp and sauté in butter. Add green onions and mushrooms, and cook 3 to 4 minutes. Add nuts. Remove from heat; add crumbs, eggs, herbs, and seasonings. Combine well. Pile into zucchini shells. Top with grated cheese. Bake in buttered baking dish in ½-inch of water, uncovered, at 350 degrees F. about 25 minutes. Makes 4 to 6 servings.

Zucchini Italian

1 pound zucchini
1 clove garlic, sliced
1 tablespoon olive oil
1 large tomato, peeled and quartered
1½ teaspoon salt
½ teaspoon oregano
Pepper to taste

Scrub zucchini with stiff brush and slice crosswise into thin slices. Sauté the garlic in the oil 1 minute in a 1½ quart pan. Stir in zucchini and remaining ingredients; cover and cook over low heat 15 minutes. Makes 4 servings.

Mock Hollandaise Sauce

¾ cup mayonnaise
¼ cup butter or margarine, softened
¼ teaspoon salt
Dash pepper
1 tablespoon lemon juice
1 teaspoon grated lemon rind (optional)

Blend mayonnaise, butter, salt, and pepper; cook over *low* heat until butter melts and mixture is hot and smooth. Add lemon juice and rind. Makes about 1 cup.

Serve on asparagus, broccoli, or poached fish, or wherever Hollandaise Sauce is called for.

Lemon Sauce

2 egg yolks
1 cup sugar
2 tablespoons cornstarch
1 cup juice (use juice from 1 orange, then fill the remainder with lemon juice)

Combine egg yolks and sugar in a small heavy saucepan. Add cornstarch, then juice, and mix well. Stir and cook until thick. Makes about 1 cup. Wonderful over broccoli.

Salads and Salad Dressings

Herbed Croutons for Salads

¼ cup grated Parmesan cheese
1 tablespoon oregano
1 tablespoon garlic powder
1 tablespoon basil
½ teaspoon salt
½ teaspoon fresh-ground pepper
1 loaf dry bread, cut in cubes (15 to 20 cups)
3 tablespoons oil

In small bowl mix Parmesan cheese, oregano, garlic powder, basil, salt, and pepper; set aside. In large bowl toss bread cubes with oil, then toss with cheese-herb mixture until well mixed. Spread on ungreased cookie sheet. Bake at 225 degrees F. for 1 hour or until crisp and lightly golden, stirring occasionally. Cool and store in a cool place, in plastic bags with tie. Will keep about 1 month. Yield: 15 to 20 cups.

Green Salad

1 large head crisped lettuce
7 green onions, chopped (use part of green tops)
¼ head red cabbage
¼ large head white cabbage
3-4 medium tomatoes, cut in wedges

Dressing

2 tablespoons mayonnaise
1 tablespoon chopped parsley
Dash of garlic salt
Juice of 1 lemon (3 tablespoons)
2 tablespoons vinegar
Salt and pepper
1 teaspoon paprika
½ cup heavy cream

Combine dressing ingredients and let stand for at least 30 minutes. Pour dressing over greens. Do not mix, but toss lightly just before serving. Garnish with tomato wedges. Makes about 12 servings.

Green Goddess Salad

1 head romaine lettuce
3 hard-cooked eggs, chopped
6 green onions, chopped
1 cup Green Goddess dressing
1 cup shrimp, fresh cooked or canned
1 cup croutons

Wash and drain lettuce; break into small pieces. Place on individual salad plates. Top with eggs and green onions. Drizzle dressing over salad, then place a few shrimp and croutons on each salad. Makes 6 salads.

Green Goddess Dressing

1 cup mayonnaise
½ cup thick sour cream
3 tablespoons tarragon vinegar
1 tablespoon lemon juice
⅓ cup finely chopped parsley
3 tablespoons finely chopped onion
3 tablespoons mashed anchovy fillets
1 tablespoon chopped chives
2 tablespoons chopped capers
1 small clove garlic, minced
¼ teaspoon pepper
½ teaspoon salt

Combine all ingredients in quart jar. Cover jar tightly and shake until mixture is well blended. Chill in refrigerator three to four hours. Shake well before using.

Salata (Greek Tossed Salad)

1 clove garlic, cut in half
½ head lettuce, torn
½ bunch endive, torn
3 tomatoes, cut in eighths (peeled if desired)
1 cucumber, peeled and sliced
6 green onions, thinly sliced
2 stalks celery, sliced
1 green pepper, slivered
2 tablespoons chopped fresh parsley
1 teaspoon oregano (optional)
1 teaspoon salt
⅛ teaspoon pepper
Olive oil
Wine vinegar
1 cooked beet, cut into shoestring strips
8 slices cheese, cut in shoestring strips (optional)
8 ripe Greek olives
¼ cup chickpeas, cooked (garbanzo beans)
2 hard-cooked eggs, quartered

Rub a wooden salad bowl with garlic halves. Discard garlic. Combine next eleven ingredients. Toss with enough oil to coat. Add ¼ as much vinegar as oil and toss lightly. Garnish as desired with remaining ingredients. Makes 6 to 8 servings.

Spinach Salad

1 pound fresh spinach
½ cup salad oil
1 clove garlic, slivered
¼ cup vinegar
¼ cup lemon juice
½ teaspoon salt
Dash pepper
2 tablespoons Parmesan cheese
2 hard-cooked eggs, sliced
6 slices crisp bacon, crumbled

Wash spinach; dry thoroughly and discard stems. Tear in pieces into salad bowl. Chill. Combine salad oil and garlic and refrigerate one hour. Discard garlic. Heat oil with vinegar, lemon juice, salt, pepper, and cheese. Toss spinach with dressing. Garnish with eggs and bacon. Makes 4 to 6 servings.

Beet Salad

1 cup cooked diced or shoestring beets
1 package (3 ounces) strawberry, cherry, or raspberry gelatin
¾ teaspoon salt
1 cup boiling water or beet juice
1 cup crushed pineapple with juice (8-ounce can)

Drain beets, measuring liquid. Add water to make 1 cup. Dissolve gelatin and salt in boiling liquid. Add 4 ice cubes and stir until ice is melted. Chill until thickened. Add beets and crushed pineapple. Chill until set. Makes 6 to 8 servings.

Dressing for Beet Salad

⅔ cup chopped celery
½ cup green onions, sliced very thin
½ cup sour cream

Fold vegetables into sour cream. Let stand to develop flavors. Serve about 1 tablespoon of dressing on each salad.

Four-Bean Salad

½ cup sugar
½ teaspoon salt
⅔ cup oil
⅔ cup vinegar
1 can (16 ounces) garbanzo beans, drained
1 can (16 ounces) green beans, drained
1 can (16 ounces) yellow wax beans, drained
1 can (16 ounces) red kidney beans, drained
1 small onion cut into rings

Combine sugar, salt, oil, and vinegar. Stir or shake until sugar is dissolved. Drain beans thoroughly and add onion rings. Pour dressing over beans and let marinate for 2 hours. Serve about one cup of mixture on each of 8 lettuce leaves. Makes 8 servings.

Evelyn's Salad

Lettuce
Ripe olives
Artichoke hearts (canned)
Tiny whole beets (canned)
Asparagus tips (canned)
French dressing

On a bed of lettuce, arrange olives, artichoke hearts, beets, and asparagus tips artistically. Pour on French dressing and serve immediately.

California Salad

2 oranges, peeled, with white membrane removed, and sliced
2 tomatoes, sliced
½ green pepper, slivered
3 green onions and tops, sliced
6 radishes, sliced
2 celery ribs, thinly sliced
1 cup shredded raw spinach

Toss ingredients together in a bowl. Just before serving, toss with dressing. Makes 6 servings.

Dressing

⅓ cup vinegar
½ cup sugar
⅔ cup water
½ teaspoon salt
Freshly ground pepper

Mix all ingredients together until sugar is dissolved thoroughly. Chill overnight.

Carrot-Pineapple-Coconut Salad

5 or 6 medium carrots, finely shredded
1 small can (8 ounces) crushed pineapple
1 cup shredded or flaked coconut
Pinch of salt

Mix all ingredients. Salad may be served with a salad dressing, if desired. Makes 4 to 6 servings.

Sarah's Salad

1 head iceberg lettuce
3 strips bacon
½ 10-ounce package frozen peas
¼ teaspoon sugar
½ teaspoon salt
¼ teaspoon pepper
½ cup shredded Swiss cheese (or cut 2½ ounces in strips)
⅔ cup chopped green onion
¼ cup mayonnaise
¼ cup salad dressing

Wash and drain lettuce. Dry thoroughly. Dice bacon and sauté until crisp; drain on paper towels. Run hot water over frozen peas and drain. Tear lettuce into bite-size pieces into salad bowl. Sprinkle with sugar, salt, and pepper. Add peas, cheese, onion, mayonnaise, and salad dressing. (These ingredients may be layered, if desired, with the mayonnaise spread on last. Cover tightly and refrigerate overnight.) Chill. Toss when ready to serve and garnish with bacon. Makes 8 servings.

Copper Penny Salad

1 can (10½ ounces) tomato soup
1 cup sugar
½ cup vinegar
½ cup salad oil
1 teaspoon salt
1 teaspoon dry mustard
4 pounds carrots, sliced and cooked
1 large onion, cut into thin rings
1 large green pepper, diced

Combine tomato soup, sugar, vinegar, salad oil, salt, and mustard in a saucepan and bring to a boil. Pour the hot dressing over carrots, onion, and green pepper. Marinate 24 hours. Serve hot or cold. Salad will keep up to two weeks in refrigerator. Makes 12 to 16 servings.

Cantaloupe Salad

2 small cantaloupes
6 peaches, peeled and sliced
2 cups honeydew melon, cubed
3 cups seeded grapes, halved
French fruit dressing (below)

Cut each cantaloupe lengthwise into 8 wedges; peel and chill. Coat peaches, honeydew melon, and grapes with dressing. (Keep remaining dressing for another use.) Chill one hour. For each serving, arrange 2 cantaloupe wedges to form oval or circle and fill centers with fruit mixture. Makes 8 servings.

French Fruit Dressing

⅓ cup sugar
1 teaspoon salt
1 teaspoon paprika
¼ cup orange juice
1 tablespoon lemon juice
1 tablespoon vinegar
1 cup salad oil
1 teaspoon onion, grated

Combine all ingredients in a bottle or jar and cover. Shake thoroughly. Store any leftover dressing in refrigerator for use another time. Shake well before each use.

Apple Salad

8 tart apples, peeled, if desired, and chopped
½ cup diced celery
½ cup chopped dates
½ cup chopped nuts
2 tablespoons lemon juice
2 tablespoons sugar
Maraschino cherries, if desired
Salad dressing or whipped cream (optional)

Combine apples, celery, dates, nuts, and lemon juice. Sprinkle with sugar; toss and chill. Serve on lettuce leaf, garnished with cherries and with a dollop of salad dressing or whipped cream, if desired. Makes 10 to 12 servings.

Cottage Cheese Fruit Salad

1 pint cottage cheese
2 cups (1-pound can) fruit cocktail with juice
1 cup mandarin oranges, drained
1 cup (about 14-ounce can) chunk pineapple, drained
1 cup miniature marshmallows or cut large marshmallows
½ cup flaked coconut
Red grapes, halved

Mix all ingredients except grapes. Put into 8x4-inch loaf pan, and chill for several hours or overnight. Slice and serve on lettuce leaf. Garnish with red grapes. Makes 7 one-cup servings. Salad recipe may be doubled for 15 servings.

Frozen Fruit Salad

1 package (3 ounces) lemon gelatin
Dash salt
1 cup boiling water
1 can (about 8 ounces) pineapple tidbits or crushed pineapple (drain and reserve juice)
¼ cup lemon juice
⅓ cup mayonnaise
1 8-ounce package cream cheese, softened
1 banana, sliced
¼ cup maraschino cherries, halved
½ cup cut seedless grapes or mandarin oranges or miniature marshmallows
¼ cup chopped nuts (optional)
½ cup heavy cream, whipped

Dissolve gelatin and salt in boiling water. Add water to pineapple juice to make ½ cup. Stir into gelatin along with lemon juice. Chill until thick and wiggly.

Blend mayonnaise and cream cheese until smooth. Fold into chilled gelatin along with fruits, nuts, and whipped cream. Pour into two freezer trays, or pack into a 9x5x3-inch loaf pan. Freeze until firm, at least 3 to 4 →

hours. To serve, cut in squares or slices. Makes about 4 cups or 8 slices.

Note: Whipped cream may replace the cream cheese; use 2 cups total (1 cup before whipping). Or use 2 cups sour cream. Other fruits may be used, using a total of about 2 cups—drained diced orange sections, drained canned fruit cocktail, etc.

Cranberry Salad

  1 cup water
  2 cups sugar
  4 cups cranberries
  2 cups miniature marshmallows, or cut large
     marshmallows
  2 apples, diced
  3 bananas, sliced
  3 cups orange sections
  ½ cup pecans

Combine water and sugar; boil until syrupy. Add cranberries and cook until cranberries burst. Remove from heat and let stand 10 minutes. Chill. Add remaining ingredients to cranberries and chill thoroughly. Serve on lettuce leaf. Top with whipped cream dressing, if desired. Makes 14 servings.

Cranberry Fluff Salad

  2 cups raw cranberries, ground
  ½ cup sugar
  2 cups diced apples, pared or unpared as desired
  ½ cup chopped walnuts
  3 cups miniature marshmallows
  ¼ teaspoon salt
  1 cup heavy cream, whipped

Combine cranberries and sugar; cover and chill overnight. Add apples, walnuts, marshmallows, and salt. Fold in whipped cream. Chill. Serve as a salad or as dessert. Makes about 12 servings.

Grapefruit Salad

  2 envelopes (2 tablespoons) gelatin
  ½ cup cold water
  1 cup boiling water
  1 cup sugar
  ½ teaspoon salt
  Juice of 1 lemon
  2 cans (16 ounces each) grapefruit and juice

Soften gelatin in cold water. Add boiling water, sugar, salt, and lemon juice. Cool. Add grapefruit. Chill until set. Serve with a dollop of dressing (below). Makes about 8 servings.

Dressing

  1½ tablespoons flour
  2 tablespoons sugar
  Pinch dry mustard
  1 tablespoon lemon juice
  1 egg, unbeaten
  1 cup pineapple juice
  1 cup heavy cream, whipped

Combine flour, sugar, mustard, lemon juice, and egg. Stir until smooth. Add pineapple juice; mix well. Cook on low heat, stirring constantly until it barely comes to a boil. Remove at once and cool. Add whipped cream. Serve on Grapefruit Salad.

Fruit Salad

  1 package (3 ounces) lemon pudding and pie
     filling
  1 can (about 16 ounces) fruit cocktail, drained
     (reserve juice)
  1 can (13¼ ounces) pineapple tidbits, drained
     (reserve juice)
  Miniature marshmallows, as desired
  1 cup heavy cream, whipped
  2 bananas

Cook pudding as directed on package, using the reserved fruit juices instead of water. Cool. Add drained fruit, marshmallows, and whipped cream. Slice bananas and add just before serving. Makes 6 to 8 servings. Also good served as a dessert.

Note: Drained mandarin oranges and fresh strawberries may be used in place of or together with the pineapple and fruit cocktail.

Six-Cup Salad

1 cup miniature marshmallows
1 cup pineapple chunks or tidbits, drained
1 cup mandarin oranges, drained
1 cup sour cream
1 cup coconut
1 cup maraschino cherry halves

In a 2-quart container mix all ingredients together carefully; chill in refrigerator from 12 to 24 hours. Spoon onto lettuce leaves. Makes 6 to 8 servings.

Strawberry-Blueberry Mold

3¾ cups water
1 large package (6 ounces) wild cherry gelatin
2 tablespoons lemon juice
1 pint fresh strawberries
1½ cups fresh blueberries or 1 package (10 ounces) frozen blueberries
2 cups seedless grapes, halved
Salad greens
French dressing
1 cup heavy cream, whipped (optional)

Heat 2 cups of the water; add flavored gelatin and stir until dissolved. Stir in the remaining 1¾ cups water and the lemon juice. Chill until syrupy.

Wash and halve the strawberries; arrange in bottom of a 3-quart ring mold, or use individual molds. Pour in enough of the chilled gelatin to cover berries; chill. Mix the remaining gelatin with blueberries and grapes; pour into mold. Chill until firm. When ready to serve, unmold on greens that have been tossed in French dressing. Serve with a dollop of sweetened whipped cream, if desired. Makes 10 to 12 servings. This may also be served as a dessert.

Pear Blush Salad

1 large can (1 pound 14 ounces) pear halves, drained
1 package (3 ounces) cream cheese, softened
¼ cup nuts, finely chopped
2 tablespoons maraschino cherry juice
Mint leaves

Combine cream cheese, enough juice from pears to soften cheese, and nuts. Put a rounded teaspoon of this mixture in the seed part of half the pears. Cover with the other pear half. Lightly brush cheeks of pear with maraschino cherry juice. (Red food coloring diluted with water may be used.) Stand pear on bed of lettuce and garnish with mint leaves. Makes 4 servings.

Princess Salad

1 can (16 ounces) pears, drained and cut
2 cups miniature marshmallows
2 cups crushed pineapple, drained
¼ cup maraschino cherries, cut
1 cup cream, whipped
½ cup chopped nuts
Lettuce

Combine pears, marshmallows, pineapple, cherries, and unsweetened whipped cream. Place on lettuce bed and sprinkle with a few nuts. Makes 8 servings.

Honey Fruit Slaw

1 small head green cabbage, shredded
1 can (8 ounces) mandarin oranges
½ cup raisins
⅓ cup chopped, blanched almonds
1 cup salad dressing
⅓ cup honey

Mix cabbage, oranges, raisins, and almonds together in a large bowl. Combine salad dressing and honey and pour over cabbage. Mix lightly and serve. Makes 12 servings.

Golden Carrot Salad

3 medium carrots, peeled and sliced
1 teaspoon French dressing
⅓ cup celery, thinly sliced
1 tablespoon small sweet pickles, sliced
1 tablespoon mayonnaise or salad dressing

Slice carrots thin and cook them in boiling salted water until tender crisp. Drain. Drizzle French dressing over carrots. Chill 1 hour. Just before serving, add the remaining ingredients. Mix lightly. Makes 6 servings.

Mandarin Salad

2 quarts salad greens torn into pieces (a variety preferred)
2 to 3 ribs celery, cut on diagonal
1 can (8 ounces) Mandarin oranges, drained
2 to 3 green onions, cut on diagonal (use some of the green top)
1 cup grapes, any variety (those with seeds should be halved and seeds removed)
½ cup pecans, coarsely cut

Clean and dry greens thoroughly. Add remaining ingredients. Toss to mix well. Just before serving, toss with dressing, using just enough to moisten lightly.

Dressing

2 tablespoons sesame seeds, toasted*
3 tablespoons sugar or honey
1 teaspoon monosodium glutamate (MSG)
1 teaspoon salt
Pepper
¼ cup salad oil
2 tablespoons vinegar

Mix all ingredients together thoroughly. Dressing may be stored in refrigerator. Shake well before using.

*To toast sesame seeds: Measure seeds onto pie pan or baking sheet and place in 350-degree F. oven for about 10 minutes. Stir occasionally. You don't want them brown, just golden.

Angel Salad

1 cup miniature marshmallows
3 bananas, chopped
1 cup (15½-ounce can) pineapple chunks, drained and chopped
½ cup peanuts, crushed
2 tablespoons cornstarch
2 tablespoons sugar
1 cup pineapple juice
1 egg, beaten lightly
½ cup cream, whipped

Mix marshmallows and fruit. Add peanuts. Make a cooked dressing of the cornstarch, sugar, juice, and egg, blended in that order. Heat, stirring constantly, until thickened. Cool and fold in whipped cream. Combine with salad mixture, just to moisten. Serve on greens. Makes 4 to 6 servings.

Fresh Fruit Mold

1 fresh grapefruit
1 envelope (1 tablespoon) unflavored gelatin
½ cup sugar
¼ teaspoon salt
¼ cup water
¼ cup fresh lemon juice
1 cup orange juice, fresh or frozen
½ cup red grapes, seeded
½ cup thinly sliced ripe banana

Peel and section grapefruit. Cut sections in thirds. Place in bowl to allow juices to accumulate. Squeeze juice from membrane into bowl before discarding.

Meanwhile, combine gelatin, sugar, and salt in a saucepan. Stir in water and lemon juice. Place over medium heat and stir constantly until gelatin is dissolved—3 to 4 minutes. Remove from heat. Drain grapefruit sections, measuring juice. Add water if necessary, to make ¼ cup. Then add orange and grapefruit juice to gelatin mixture. Chill until slightly thickened.

Fold in fruits. Pour into a 3-cup mold. Chill until firm—at least 2 hours. Makes 3 cups or 6 servings.

Lime Gelatin, Shrimp, and Grapefruit Salad

1 large package (6 ounces) lime gelatin
1 cup boiling water
6 to 8 ice cubes
2 tablespoons sliced olives
1 tablespoon sweet pickle relish
½ tablespoon minced onions
1 teaspoon prepared mustard
1 teaspoon vinegar
¾ cup shrimp
1½ cups grapefruit sections, drained
3 tablespoons chopped green peppers
¼ cup heavy cream, whipped
¼ cup mayonnaise

Make up gelatin according to package directions, using boiling water and ice cubes for the ice cube method. Cool until syrupy. Add remaining ingredients except mayonnaise and cream.

Pour into 1½-quart mold or 8 individual molds. Chill until firm. Unmold or cut and serve on lettuce leaves. Top with a dollop of mayonnaise, or mayonnaise fluffed with whipped cream, if desired. Makes 8 servings.

Raspberry Gelatin Salad

1 small package (3 ounces) raspberry gelatin
1¼ cups boiling water
1 package (10 ounces) frozen raspberries (not thawed)
1 cup crushed pineapple, with juice
1 large banana, sliced
½ cup pecans
1 cup sour cream

Pour boiling water over gelatin. Stir for 2 minutes to dissolve thoroughly. Add raspberries, pineapple, banana, and pecans. Pour into individual molds and chill until firm; unmold onto lettuce leaves and garnish with sour cream. Makes 8 to 10 servings.

Crab and Avocado Salad

3 large avocados, peeled, pitted, cut into cubes
2 cans (about 7 ounces each) crab meat, rinsed and drained well and picked over to remove pieces of cartilage
1 cup finely diced celery
½ cup finely sliced radishes
2 tablespoons lemon juice
2 tablespoons vinegar
4 tablespoons salad oil
2 tablespoons finely chopped green onions (use part of green tops)
Dash of cayenne pepper
Salt to taste
3 or 4 tomatoes (optional)

Combine the above ingredients (except tomatoes). For each serving, spoon out salad on a bed of lettuce on individual serving plates. Surround with tomato wedges, peeled if desired. Serve with Louis dressing (below). Makes 6 servings.

Louis Dressing

1 cup mayonnaise
⅓ cup chili sauce
2 tablespoons chopped parsley
1 tablespoon finely chopped green onion
Dash of cayenne pepper
¼ cup heavy cream, whipped

Combine first 5 ingredients; fold in whipped cream. Top each salad with 3 to 4 tablespoons dressing. Pass remainder for those who wish extra dressing.

Shrimp Salad

3 cans (5 ounces each) shrimp
1 cup chopped celery
¼ cup sliced stuffed olives
2 tablespoons lemon juice
3 hard-cooked eggs, cut in wedges
1 avocado, peeled and cut in wedges
¼ cup coarsely chopped cashews (optional) ↗

Combine shrimp, celery, olives, and lemon juice. Blend dressing ingredients thoroughly. When ready to serve, toss dressing (below) with salad. Garnish with hard-cooked eggs, avocado, and cashews. Makes 6 to 8 servings.

Dressing

> 1 cup mayonnaise
> ⅓ cup chili sauce
> 1 teaspoon grated onion

Mix ingredients together. Toss with shrimp salad.

Cranberry Set Salad

> 1 large package (6 ounces) cherry-flavored gelatin
> 2 cups hot water
> 2 cups chipped ice (or use 4 to 6 large ice cubes)

Combine gelatin and hot water; stir until gelatin is completely dissolved. Cool with ice. Chill. When partially set, add:

> 1 can (16 ounces) jellied cranberry sauce
> ¼ teaspoon salt
> ½ cup sugar

Whip cranberry mixture until smooth and add:

> 1 large apple, diced
> ½ cup walnuts, chopped
> 1 small can crushed pineapple (do not drain)

Chill until set. Serve on lettuce leaf topped with whipped cream, if desired. Makes 10 to 12 servings.

Tuna Mold

> 1 envelope (1 tablespoon) unflavored gelatin
> ¼ cup cold water
> 2 vegetable or chicken bouillon cubes
> 1 cup boiling water

> 2 cups mayonnaise
> 2 cans (7 ounces each) tuna,* drained and flaked
> 2 hard-cooked eggs, chopped
> ⅓ cup chopped stuffed olives
> ⅓ cup chopped ripe olives
> 1 tablespoon finely chopped green onions or chives

Add gelatin to cold water; let stand about 5 minutes. Dissolve bouillon cubes in boiling water in a large bowl. Add gelatin and stir until completely dissolved. Add mayonnaise and blend well. Chill until slightly thickened. Then add remaining ingredients. Blend well. Pour into a 2-quart mold or individual molds. Chill until firm, about 3 hours. Unmold and serve on greens. Makes about 6 cups or 10 to 12 servings.

*Or use 2 cans chicken, chopped, or about 2 cups cooked chicken.

Chicken Curry Salad with Fruit

> ⅔ cup mayonnaise
> 2 tablespoons lemon juice
> 1 teaspoon salt
> 1 teaspoon curry powder
> 2½ cups cooked chicken, diced
> 1 cup diced celery
> Salad greens
> ¼ cup slivered blanched almonds
> 1 avocado, sliced
> ½ cantaloupe, cut into wedges
> 1 cup seedless grapes
> 1 cup canned pineapple chunks, drained

Blend mayonnaise, lemon juice, salt, and curry powder. Pour over the combined chicken and celery and mix lightly. Chill. Just before serving, mound salad in center of a serving platter lined with salad greens. Sprinkle with almonds. Garnish with avocado and fruits. Makes 6 servings.

Pear and Lime Salad or Dessert

1 can (16 ounces) pear halves
1 small package (3 ounces) lime gelatin
1 cup boiling water
1 cup pear syrup and water
1 tablespoon lemon juice
1 package (3 ounces) cream cheese
1 to 2 tablespoons finely chopped nuts

Drain pears, measuring syrup. Add water to syrup to make 1 cup. Place pears, cut side up, in 8-inch square pan. Dissolve gelatin in boiling water. Add measured syrup and water and lemon juice; pour over pears. Chill until firm—about 3 hours. Divide cheese into 6 pieces. Roll each into a ball; then roll in nuts. Cut gelatin into 6 servings; garnish with cheese balls. Serve on lettuce for salad. Makes 6 servings.

Orange Cream Fruit Salad

1 can (15 ounces) pineapple chunks, drained
1 cup peach slices, drained
1 can (8 ounces) mandarin oranges, drained
1 large banana, sliced
1 small apple, cut in chunks
3 tablespoons frozen orange-juice concentrate
3 tablespoons milk
2 tablespoons sour cream
1 package (6 ounces) instant vanilla pudding
Lettuce

Combine fruits and mix lightly. Combine orange juice, milk, sour cream, and pudding mix. Fold into fruit mixture. Cover and refrigerate several hours. Serve in a lettuce cup. Makes 6 to 8 servings.

Dreamy Fruit Salad

2 cans (15 ounces each) pineapple tidbits
2 cans (8 ounces each) mandarin oranges
4 bananas
1 pound seedless green grapes
1 package (10 ½ ounces) colored miniature marshmallows
1 cup shredded coconut
2 cups (16 ounces) sour cream

Drain pineapple and mandarin oranges well. Combine all fruits, marshmallows, and coconut. Fold in sour cream. Chill several hours before serving. Makes 12 servings.

Apple Valley Salad

½ head green cabbage, shredded
2 red apples, diced (leave skins on)
½ cup chopped green onions
1 medium green pepper, slivered
1 teaspoon sugar
1 teaspoon seasoning salt
¼ teaspoon pepper
1 cup mayonnaise
½ cup sugar
⅓ cup vinegar

Toss cabbage, apples, green onions, and green peppers together in a large bowl. Sprinkle with 1 teaspoon sugar, seasoning salt, and pepper. Combine mayonnaise, ½ cup sugar, and vinegar, and pour over cabbage mixture. Toss lightly. To serve, garnish with red apple slices. Serves 12.

Calico Tossed Salad

1 small head romaine lettuce
1 carrot, sliced thin
⅛ head red cabbage, chopped
1 tablespoon chopped green onion
1 package (10 ounces) frozen peas, thawed
3 hard-cooked eggs, peeled and sliced

Wash romaine and tear into bite-size pieces. In a large salad bowl place romaine, carrots, cabbage, green onion, and peas. Toss lightly. Just before serving add cherry tomatoes and slices of hard-cooked eggs. Makes 8 to 10 servings.

Stuffed Tomatoes with Egg Salad

6 large tomatoes
10 hard-cooked eggs
½ cup chopped green pepper
⅓ cup chopped green onions
1 cup chopped celery
¾ cup salad dressing
½ teaspoon salt
Dash of pepper
½ teaspoon prepared mustard
1 head lettuce
Orange slices
Avocado slices

Wash and core tomatoes. Carefully cut each into sixths, leaving a hinge at the bottom. Peel hard-cooked eggs and chop very fine or grind in food grinder. Mix eggs, green pepper, chopped green onions, celery, salad dressing, salt, pepper, and mustard until well blended. Arrange a lettuce cup on each plate. Place a tomato in each lettuce cup, and scoop ½ cup of egg salad mixture in middle of tomato. Garnish each serving with an orange slice and an avocado slice. Makes 6 servings.

Tomato Coleslaw

1 head green cabbage, ground or chopped coarsely
1 small green pepper, chopped
3 green onions, chopped
1 ripe tomato, diced
½ carrot, grated fine
1 cup mayonnaise
2 tablespoons vinegar
¼ cup sugar
1 teaspoon celery seed
1 teaspoon salt
½ teaspoon pepper
Lettuce
Tomato for garnish

Combine cabbage, green pepper, onions, tomato, and carrot in a large bowl and toss lightly. Mix mayonnaise, vinegar, sugar, celery seed, salt, and pepper in a small bowl and stir until blended. Pour dressing over vegetables and toss lightly. Cover and refrigerate several hours. To serve individual salads, scoop onto lettuce leaf and garnish with a slice of tomato. Makes about 12 servings.

Mexican Taco Salad

2 pounds ground beef
1 cup chopped onions
1 can (30 ounces) refried beans
1 can (15 ounces) tomato sauce
1 package taco seasoning
⅛ teaspoon Tabasco sauce
Salt and pepper to taste
1 head lettuce, shredded
1 package (16 ounces) corn chips
½ pound Cheddar cheese, grated
4 tomatoes, diced
1 bunch green onions, chopped
1 cup (8 ounces) sour cream
1 cup guacamole

Brown ground beef in a heavy skillet. Drain off fat. Add onions and cook until tender. Add refried beans, tomato sauce, taco seasoning, Tabasco sauce, salt, and pepper. Simmer until flavors are blended. To serve: Place a bed of shredded lettuce on each plate. Circle with corn chips. Spoon on 3 or 4 tablespoons of meat mixture. Top with grated cheese, diced tomatoes, chopped green onions, and a spoonful each of sour cream and guacamole. Serves 12.

Cucumber Set Salad

1 large package (6 ounces) lime gelatin
1½ cups hot water
½ cup lemon juice
2 teaspoons onion juice
Dash of garlic salt
Dash of cayenne pepper
1 cup mayonnaise
2 cups chopped unpeeled cucumber
¼ cup red pepper or pimiento, chopped

Dissolve gelatin in hot water. Add lemon juice, onion juice, garlic salt, and cayenne pepper. Chill until partially set. Fold in mayonnaise, cucumbers, and red pepper. Pour into individual molds or a 2-quart mold and chill until firm. Makes 12 to 14 servings.

Thousand Island Dressing

1½ cups salad dressing
¼ cup pickle relish
⅓ cup chili sauce
⅓ cup milk (or to make desired consistency)

Combine ingredients; mix well, then chill. Stir before serving. Makes 2 cups.

Boiled Salad Dressing

1 tablespoon salt
2 teaspoons dry mustard

6 tablespoons sugar
Few grains cayenne pepper
1 teaspoon celery seed
1 tablespoon flour
4 egg yolks
3 tablespoons margarine, melted
1½ cups milk
½ cup vinegar

Combine all ingredients except vinegar, and cook over low heat until mixture thickens, stirring constantly. Add vinegar, blend well, and chill. Makes about one quart. Will keep about two months in refrigerator. This is a very good coleslaw dressing.

Buttermilk Dressing No. 1

1½ cups mayonnaise
¼ cup buttermilk (more may be used, depending on consistency desired)
½ teaspoon monosodium glutamate (MSG)
½ teaspoon salt, or to taste
Pepper to taste
¼ teaspoon onion salt
¼ teaspoon garlic salt
2 tablespoons fresh chopped parsley

Combine all ingredients. Let stand one-half day before using. Crumbled blue cheese may be added. Makes about 2 cups.

Buttermilk Dressing No. 2

2 cups mayonnaise
2 cups buttermilk
1 package (8 ounces) cream cheese
1 teaspoon onion salt
1 teaspoon garlic salt
¼ teaspoon ground pepper, or to taste
¼ teaspoon monosodium glutamate (MSG)

Combine all ingredients; let stand to blend flavors. Serve as salad dressing, dip, or sauce over baked potatoes.

Russian Dressing

1 cup sugar
1 cup catsup
1 cup vinegar
1 cup oil
1 teaspoon mustard
¼ teaspoon pepper
½ cup finely chopped onion
1 tablespoon lemon juice
½ teaspoon Worcestershire sauce

Mix ingredients in blender; chill. Makes about 1 quart. Store in refrigerator.

Strawberry Dressing for Fruit Salad

1 package (10 ounces) frozen strawberries, thawed and drained
⅔ cup mayonnaise
1 carton (8 ounces) strawberry-flavored yogurt

Combine strawberries and mayonnaise, then fold in yogurt. Cover and chill for 1 hour. Serve over fresh fruit, honeydew wedges, and strawberries. Garnish with mint. Makes 3 cups.

Sour Cream Herb Dressing

1 cup sour cream
2 tablespoons vinegar
1 teaspoon sugar
½ teaspoon salt
½ teaspoon celery seed
Dash of pepper
¼ teaspoon crumbled dried thyme

Blend all ingredients together. Chill. Makes about 1 cup.

Frozen Blue Cheese Dressing

1 package (3 ounces) cream cheese, softened
⅓ cup mayonnaise or salad dressing

1 tablespoon lemon juice
4 ounces blue cheese, crumbled
⅔ cup chopped celery
¼ teaspoon salt
½ cup heavy cream, whipped

Combine the first 3 ingredients; beat until fluffy. Add blue cheese, celery, and salt. Fold in whipped cream. Freeze in refrigerator trays. Cut into cubes. Serve a cube on top of each fruit salad.

Blue Cheese Dressing

2 cups mayonnaise
1 small onion, grated
4 tablespoons cider vinegar
Dash garlic salt
1 cup sour cream
¾ cup chopped fresh parsley
3 ounces (or more) blue cheese

Combine all ingredients except cheese and mix well. Crumble the blue cheese in last. Makes about 1 quart dressing.

Celery Seed Fruit Salad Dressing

½ cup sugar
1 teaspoon salt
1 teaspoon mustard
1 teaspoon celery seed
1 teaspoon paprika
1 cup salad oil
¼ cup vinegar

Mix sugar and seasonings. Gradually add salad oil and vinegar alternately. Beat well with rotary beater after each addition. Makes 1⅔ cups.

Mustard Cream

3 tablespoons dry mustard
2 tablespoons sugar
1 tablespoon cornstarch
1 teaspoon salt
1 egg yolk
½ cup water
1 tablespoon butter or margarine
¼ cup white vinegar
¼ cup heavy cream, whipped

Mix mustard, sugar, cornstarch, and salt in a small saucepan. Beat egg yolk slightly with water in a cup; stir into the mustard mixture. Cook, stirring constantly, over low heat until mixture thickens and boils 3 minutes. Remove from heat; stir in butter and vinegar. Strain into a small bowl; cool.

Beat cream until stiff in a small bowl; fold into cooled mustard mixture. Chill until serving time. Makes about 1 cup. Good on coleslaw.

Poppy Seed Dressing

¾ cup sugar
1 tablespoon dry mustard
½ teaspoon salt
⅓ cup cider vinegar
1 tablespoon onion juice
1 cup salad oil
1½ tablespoons poppy seeds

Combine sugar, mustard, salt, vinegar, and onion juice in medium-size bowl. Beat oil in gradually, using portable mixer, until mixture is thick and smooth. Stir in poppy seeds and store, covered, in refrigerator. Makes 1⅔ cups.

Famous Fruit Salad Dressing

⅓ cup sugar
1 teaspoon flour
1 egg yolk
½ cup canned pineapple juice or orange juice
2 tablespoons lemon juice
1 teaspoon celery seed (optional)
½ cup heavy cream, whipped

Combine sugar, flour, egg yolk, and pineapple juice in a small saucepan; stir until smooth. Cook over low heat until thickened, stirring constantly. Add lemon juice and celery seed; chill. Fold in whipped cream just before serving. Makes about 2 cups.

Lion House French Dressing

Ingredients	1 quart	2 quarts
Sugar	1 cup	2 cups
Catsup	1 cup	2 cups
Vinegar	1 cup	2 cups
Oil	1 cup	2 cups
Mustard	1 teaspoon	2 teaspoons
Pepper	¼ teaspoon	¼ teaspoon
Onion, chopped	½ cup	1 cup
Lemon juice	1½ teaspoons	1½ tablespoons
Worcestershire sauce	½ teaspoon	1 teaspoon

Ingredients	1 gallon	2 gallons
Sugar	4 cups	8 cups
Catsup	4 cups	8 cups
Vinegar	4 cups	8 cups
Oil	4 cups	8 cups
Mustard	4 teaspoons	8 teaspoons
Pepper	½ teaspoon	¾ teaspoon
Onion, chopped	2 cups	4 cups
Lemon juice	3 tablespoons	6 tablespoons
Worcestershire	2 teaspoons	4 teaspoons

Combine ingredients and mix or shake well.

Breads and Rolls

Honey Butter

½ cup butter or margarine
¼ teaspoon vanilla
1 egg yolk
1 cup honey

Whip softened butter or margarine. Add vanilla and egg yolk. Add honey gradually while whipping. Makes 1 cup.

Whole Wheat Bread

1 package (1 tablespoon) dry yeast
3 cups lukewarm water
1 cup white flour
1 cup oatmeal
¼ cup molasses
6 tablespoons nonfat dry milk
6 tablespoons shortening, softened
6½ cups whole wheat flour
1½ tablespoons salt

Instructions for Mixing with Electric Mixer

Soften yeast in 3 cups lukewarm water in large mixing bowl. Add remaining ingredients and beat until dough forms a ball and leaves sides of bowl (part of the flour may need to be mixed in by hand). Remove beaters, cover bowl, and let dough rise for 1 hour in warm area away from drafts. Mix down and mold into 2 loaves. Place in greased bread pans and let rise until about double in size. Bake at 400 degrees F. for 30 minutes or until desired doneness. Makes 2 loaves.

Instructions for Hand Mixing

Dissolve yeast in ¼ cup lukewarm water. Combine remaining 2¾ cups water, oatmeal, molasses, and nonfat dry milk; add half of the white flour and half of the whole wheat flour, one cup at a time, beating well after each addition. Add yeast, the remaining flour, shortening, and salt. Mix well, then knead until dough is smooth and elastic. Place in a covered bowl in a warm area until double in bulk. Knead for one minute to force out air bubbles. Mold into two loaves. Place in 2 well-greased bread pans. Cover and let rise until double in size. Bake at 400 degrees F. for 30 minutes. Remove from pans to cool. Brush tops of loaves with butter.

Dinner Rolls

2 tablespoons dry yeast (2 packets)
2 cups warm water (110-115 degrees F.)
⅓ cup sugar
⅓ cup shortening (butter, margarine, or vegetable shortening)
2½ teaspoons salt
⅔ cup nonfat dry milk
5 to 6 cups flour
1 egg

In the large bowl of an electric mixer, combine yeast and water. Let stand 5 minutes. Add sugar, shortening, salt, dry milk, 2 cups flour, and egg. Beat together until very smooth. Add 2 more cups flour, one at a time, and beat until smooth.

Add about one more cup flour, ½ cup at a time (in your mixer if it will take it, or by hand), until it is well mixed in. Turn dough onto a lightly floured board and knead until it is smooth and satiny. Gather dough into a ball. Scrape bowl clean and grease it with shortening. Return dough to bowl and grease surface lightly. Let rise away from drafts in a warm (not hot) place until about triple in bulk. (In a cool oven with a pan of hot water on a rack under it is a good place.)

Use last of the flour as needed on the board for rolling and shaping the dough. (Don't use it all unless you need it.) Let dough rest on board for 10 minutes so it will be easier to manage if you roll it. Cut or mold into desired shapes. Place on greased baking sheets. Brush surface of rolls with melted butter. Let rise in warm place until ready for oven (about 1½ hours). Bake at 400 degrees F. for 15 to 20 minutes, or until browned to your satisfaction. Makes about 3 dozen rolls.

Note: The entire mixing process may be done by hand. It takes thorough beating and kneading to develop the gluten in the dough. Soft dough makes lighter, more tender rolls. This small version of the Lion House recipe makes a soft dough, but one that can be handled. Any soft dough can be managed more easily if it is refrigerated overnight before rolling and shaping. Always add flour gradually, and keep dough as soft as you can handle it.

Banana Nut Bread

½ cup margarine
1 cup sugar
2 eggs
1 cup mashed bananas
¼ cup milk
1 teaspoon lemon juice
2 cups flour
1½ teaspoons baking powder
½ teaspoon baking soda
¼ teaspoon salt
½ cup chopped nuts

Cream margarine and sugar. Add eggs and beat. Add bananas, milk, and lemon juice. Sift dry ingredients and add. Add nuts. Bake in well-greased 8x4x3-inch loaf pan for 1 hour at 350 degrees F. Makes 1 loaf.

Cranberry Bread

2 cups flour
1 teaspoon salt
½ teaspoon baking powder
½ teaspoon baking soda
1 cup sugar
1 egg, beaten
2 tablespoons hot water
2 tablespoons melted shortening
½ cup orange juice
½ cup chopped nuts
1 cup cut fresh cranberries
Grated rind from one orange

Sift flour, salt, baking powder, baking soda, and sugar together. Combine egg, water, shortening, and orange juice. Add to dry ingredients and mix until just blended. Fold in nuts, cranberries, and orange rind. Bake in a well-greased loaf pan (8x4x3-inch) at 325 degrees F. for about one hour, or until loaf tests done. Cool, wrap in plastic or foil wrap, and place in refrigerator 24 hours before slicing. Makes one loaf.

Date Nut Bread

1½ cups water   1 egg, beaten well
1 cup chopped dates   2¼ cups flour
2 teaspoons baking soda   1 cup chopped nuts
1 tablespoon shortening, melted
¾ cup sugar
½ teaspoon salt
¼ teaspoon baking powder
1 teaspoon vanilla

Simmer water and dates together for 3 minutes. Cool slightly, then add soda. Combine remaining ingredients except nuts; mix until smooth. Add date mixture and nuts. Blend well.

Pour into two medium loaf pans (8x4x3), which have been greased and lightly floured. Bake at 350 degrees F. for about one hour, or until loaf tests done. Remove from oven and let stand in pan for ten minutes. Turn out onto rack to complete cooling. Makes two loaves.

Orange Nut Bread

1 medium orange
1 cup raisins or dates
2 tablespoons melted butter or margarine
1 teaspoon vanilla
1 egg, beaten
2 cups flour
½ teaspoon salt
1 teaspoon baking powder
½ teaspoon baking soda
1 cup sugar
1 cup chopped nuts

Wash orange; squeeze juice. Pour juice into a one-cup measure and fill cup with boiling water. Put orange rind and raisins through chopper. (Raisins may be left whole if desired.) Combine butter, vanilla, egg, and juice-water mixture; pour onto chopped fruits. Sift dry ingredients together and add to fruit mixture. Stir in nuts last. Pour into well-greased 8x4x3-inch loaf pan. Bake 1 hour at 350 degrees F.

Note: If orange has a thick skin, remove as much of the white part under the skin as possible before grinding.

Rich Corn Bread

1 cup flour
1 cup cornmeal
1 teaspoon salt
4 teaspoons baking powder
4 eggs
½ cup sour cream
1 can (1 pound) cream-style corn
2 tablespoons salad oil
¾ cup grated cheese

Sift dry ingredients; set aside. Beat eggs until light. Add sour cream, corn, and salad oil. Stir in dry ingredients and beat well. Pour into well-greased loaf pan (8x4x2½-inch) or square pan (8x8-inch). Sprinkle with grated cheese. Bake at 400 degrees F. for 30 minutes.

Applesauce Fruit Loaf

1 cup flour
¾ pound candied fruit mixture
½ cup chopped dates
¼ cup butter
½ cup sugar
1 teaspoon baking soda
¾ cup applesauce
¼ teaspoon cloves
½ teaspoon cinnamon
¼ teaspoon salt
1 egg, beaten
1 cup seedless raisins
½ cup chopped nut meats

Add flour to candied fruit and dates. Cream butter and sugar together. Add soda to applesauce; combine with butter and sugar mixture, then add spices, salt, and egg. Combine this mixture with the fruit-flour mixture. Stir in raisins and nuts. Bake in a well-greased loaf pan (8x4x3-inch) at 300 degrees F. for 1 hour, or until it tests done. Makes 1 loaf.

Quick Bran Muffin Mix

4 cups sifted flour
2½ tablespoons baking powder
2 teaspoons salt
1 cup sugar
1 cup vegetable shortening (room temperature)
4 cups bran breakfast cereal (All Bran, Bran Buds, Bran Flakes, or Raisin Bran may be used)

Sift together flour, baking powder, salt, and sugar into large mixing bowl. Add shortening. Mix with pastry blender, fork, or slow speed of electric mixer until well blended. Stir in bran. Store in tightly covered jar until ready to use. Enough mix for 3 dozen muffins.

For 8 Muffins

2 cups Quick Bran Muffin Mix
⅔ cup milk
1 egg

Measure mix lightly in mixing bowl. Add egg to milk, and beat well. Add to mix. Stir only until combined. Fill well-greased muffin pans about ⅔ full. Bake at 400 degrees F. about 25 minutes.

Refrigerator Bran Muffins

2 cups boiling water
4 cups bran cereal (see note)
1 pound dates, pitted and chopped (see note)
1 cup salad oil
2 cups sugar
4 eggs, beaten
5 cups flour (see note)
1 teaspoon salt
5 teaspoons baking soda
1 quart buttermilk
2 cups bran flakes cereal (see note)

Pour boiling water over 4 cups of bran and dates. Sift together dry ingredients. Cream together oil and sugar. Add eggs, hot bran mixture, dry ingredients, and buttermilk. Last of all add the 2 cups of bran flakes cereal. Mix just enough to combine.

Bake in greased and floured muffin tins at 400 degrees F. for 15 to 20 minutes. Recipe makes 6 dozen muffins, but batter may be stored in a covered container in refrigerator up to 6 weeks, and any amount baked as desired.

Note: Bran Buds, All Bran, Bran Flakes, or Raisin Bran may be used; or use part all-bran and part flaked bran. Raisins may be used instead of dates. Use about 2 cups, or less if Raisin Bran is the cereal. Part whole wheat flour can be used.

Orange Rolls

1 recipe Dinner Rolls or Refrigerator Rolls
¼ cup softened butter or margarine
½ cup sugar
1 tablespoon water or orange juice
½ teaspoon orange extract or 1 teaspoon grated orange rind
Orange food coloring (1 drop red food coloring to 3 drops yellow), if desired

Follow directions for Dinner Rolls or Refrigerator Rolls. When dough is ready to shape into rolls, punch down and divide in half. Roll each half into large rectangle (about 9x13 inches, ¼-inch thick). Spread each rectangle with half of the softened butter. Combine remaining ingredients and spread over buttered dough. Starting with the long side, roll up jelly-roll style. Seal edges well, then cut with a sharp knife into 1-inch slices. Twist and stretch each slice, then place on well-greased baking sheet. Let rise away from draft until double in bulk (about 1 hour). Bake at 350 degrees F. about 20 minutes or until nicely browned. Remove rolls from pans and cool on wire rack. When rolls are cool, drizzle with Orange Glaze: Mix together 1½ cups powdered sugar, 3 tablespoons water combined with ¼ teaspoon orange extract (or use orange juice in place of the water), and ½ teaspoon grated orange rind.

Dilly Casserole Bread

1 package dry yeast
¼ cup lukewarm water
1 cup creamed cottage cheese (heated to lukewarm)
2 tablespoons sugar
1 tablespoon instant minced onion, or 2 tablespoons finely chopped fresh onion
1 tablespoon butter or margarine
2 teaspoons dill seed
1 teaspoon salt
¼ teaspoon baking soda
1 unbeaten egg
2¼ to 2½ cups all-purpose flour

Soften yeast in water. Combine in mixing bowl cottage cheese, sugar, onion, butter, dill seed, salt, soda, egg, and softened yeast. Add flour to form a stiff dough, beating well after each addition. Cover. Let rise in warm place, 85 to 90 degrees F., until light and double in bulk (about 50 to 60 minutes).

Stir dough down. Turn into well-greased, 8-inch round, 1½- or 2-quart casserole. Let rise in warm place until light, 30 to 40 minutes. Bake at 350 degrees F. for 40 to 50 minutes, until golden brown. Brush with soft butter and sprinkle with salt. Makes one round loaf.

Zucchini Bread

1 cup oil
2 cups sugar
3 eggs
3 teaspoons vanilla
2 cups shredded raw zucchini
3 cups flour
1 teaspoon soda
1 teaspoon salt
3 teaspoons cinnamon
¼ teaspoon baking powder
½ cup chopped nuts

Combine oil, sugar, and eggs in large mixer bowl. Beat well. Blend in vanilla and zucchini. Sift dry ingredients together. Add to oil mixture and blend well. Add nuts.

Pour batter into 2 loaf pans (8x4x3), well greased and lightly floured. Bake at 350 degrees F. for about 1 hour, or until loaves test done. Or use 3 medium loaf pans and reduce baking time to about 30 minutes. Let stand in pans for ten minutes, then turn out on racks to cool.

Buttermilk Scones

1 quart buttermilk
2 packages (2 tablespoons) dry yeast
¼ cup lukewarm water
¼ cup sugar
2 eggs, beaten
2 tablespoons oil
1½ teaspoons salt
3 teaspoons baking powder
½ teaspoon baking soda
8 cups flour
Cooking oil or shortening for frying

Heat buttermilk until warm. Soften yeast in lukewarm water. In a large bowl combine buttermilk, sugar, eggs, oil, salt, baking powder, baking soda, and 4 cups of the flour. Add yeast. Beat until smooth. Add remaining flour to make soft dough. Allow to rise, covered, until double in bulk. Punch down and place in refrigerator overnight.

When ready to fry, heat oil or shortening to 375 degrees F. Roll dough out on a floured board. Cut into squares about 2x2 inches. Stretch out each piece a little and drop into hot fat. Fry on one side until golden; turn and fry on the other side. Drain on paper towels. Serve hot with honey butter.

This recipe makes approximately 60 to 100 scones, depending on the size. The dough will keep in the refrigerator for 3 to 4 days. Keep punching down and cover tightly with foil or a damp cloth.

Refrigerator Rolls

¼ cup butter or margarine
¼ cup sugar
1 cup milk, scalded
1 package (1 tablespoon) dry yeast
1 tablespoon sugar
¼ cup lukewarm water
2 teaspoons salt
4 cups flour
3 eggs

Add butter and ¼ cup sugar to hot milk. Cool. Combine yeast, 1 tablespoon sugar, and lukewarm water. Let stand 5 minutes to soften yeast.

Add salt to flour. Combine milk and yeast mixtures, and add 1 cup flour. Add eggs and beat well. Continue adding flour gradually, beating until smooth after each addition. This is a soft dough, and most or all of the flour can be handled by the electric mixer.

Cover bowl and place out of draft until dough rises about triple in amount. Punch down. Cover again and place in refrigerator overnight, or until thoroughly chilled. When ready for use (dough will keep well up to 5 days) remove from refrigerator and roll and shape while cold. (You can handle a much softer dough if it is chilled.) Place on greased pans. Brush dough with melted butter. Let rolls rise 1 to 1½ hours.

Bake rolls at 375 degrees F. for 10 to 15 minutes or until desired doneness.

This dough can be left to rise for 5 to 6 hours without doing it any harm. It's a good recipe to use for church suppers or parties when you don't know how long rolls will have to stand before you can bake them.

Pumpkin Bread

1⅓ cups sugar
⅓ cup shortening
2 eggs, well beaten
1 cup pumpkin
1¾ cups flour
½ teaspoon baking soda
1 teaspoon baking powder
½ teaspoon cinnamon
¼ teaspoon cloves
½ teaspoon salt
⅓ cup hot water
⅓ cup chopped dates
⅓ cup raisins
⅓ cup chopped nuts

Cream sugar and shortening until fluffy. Add eggs and pumpkin. Sift dry ingredients together and add to the mixture. Pour hot water over dates and raisins. Add to pumpkin mixture. Add nuts. Pour into greased and lightly floured 9x5x3-inch loaf pan. Bake at 350 degrees F. for 1 hour or until bread tests done. Makes 1 large loaf.

Lion House Fruit Muffins

⅔ cup sugar
⅓ cup shortening
1 egg
¼ cup honey
1 cup milk
2 cups flour
1 teaspoon baking soda
1 teaspoon baking powder
1 teaspoon salt
½ cup drained canned fruit, in small pieces

Cream sugar and shortening together. Add egg and mix well. Add honey and milk, taking care to scrape the bowl often. Add sifted dry ingredients and mix at low speed just until blended. Fold in drained fruit. Fill greased muffin tins ¾ full. Bake at 375 degrees F. for 20 minutes. Makes 1 dozen muffins.

Cakes, Cake Desserts, and Cookies

Sting of the Bee Cake

Bienenstich Cake

1 cup butter (no substitutes)
⅔ cup sugar
2 eggs
3 cups sifted flour
3 teaspoons baking powder
1 teaspoon salt
½ cup milk

Topping

½ cup butter
1 cup finely chopped almonds, blanched or
  unblanched
½ cup sugar
2 tablespoons milk
2 teaspoons vanilla

Butter Cream Filling

1 cup butter
2 egg yolks
2 cups powdered sugar
2 teaspoons vanilla
½ cup raspberry jam

Cake: Cream butter. Gradually add sugar, creaming well. Beat in eggs one at a time; beat until light and fluffy. Add sifted dry ingredients alternately with milk. Spoon batter into a well-greased 9-inch springform pan.

Topping: Melt butter; blend in chopped almonds, sugar, milk, and vanilla. Bring to a boil. Remove from heat and cool slightly. Spread carefully over batter.

Bake at 375 degrees F. for 50 minutes. Remove from oven and cool. Remove springform pan. Prepare filling.

Filling: Soften butter. Beat in egg yolks, powdered sugar, and vanilla.

Split cake horizontally into two layers. Spread bottom layer with butter cream filling. Top with raspberry jam. Very carefully replace top layer of cake. Cut into thin slices and serve. Makes 16 to 20 servings.

Carrot Cake

1 cup sugar
½ cup oil
2 eggs, beaten
1½ cups grated carrots
1 cup unsifted flour
½ teaspoon salt
1 teaspoon baking soda
1 teaspoon cinnamon
¼ cup each ground coconut, nuts, and raisins

Combine sugar and oil. Add eggs. Mix well. Add grated carrots. Slowly stir in sifted dry ingredients. Add ground coconut, nuts, and raisins. Pour batter into lightly greased and floured 9x9-inch square cake pan. Bake at 400 degrees F. for 20 to 30 minutes, or until it tests done. When cool, spread with Frosting (below).

Frosting

1 package (8 ounces) cream cheese, softened
¼ cup margarine
2½ cups powdered sugar
2 tablespoons chopped maraschino cherries
Hot water, if needed

Cream together cream cheese, margarine, and sugar. Add cherries. Add a little hot water, 1 teaspoon at a time, until you reach spreading consistency. Mix well.

Oatmeal Cake

1½ cups boiling water
1 cup rolled oats
½ cup shortening
1 cup brown sugar
1 cup sugar
2 eggs, well beaten
1½ cups flour
1 teaspoon cinnamon
½ teaspoon nutmeg
1 teaspoon baking soda
½ teaspoon salt

Pour boiling water over oats and let stand until cool. Cream shortening with sugars and eggs until fluffy. Add oats and water mixture. Sift flour with other dry ingredients and blend into creamed mixture. Pour into greased and lightly floured 13x9x2-inch baking pan. Bake at 350 degrees F. for 35 to 45 minutes or until cake tests done. Spread topping (below) on baked cake as soon as it comes from oven.

Topping

½ cup butter or margarine
1 cup brown sugar
⅓ cup evaporated milk
1 cup coconut
1 cup nuts, chopped
1 teaspoon vanilla

Melt butter and add sugar. Blend. Add remaining ingredients and spread on baked hot cake. Place under broiler for a minute or two, if desired.

German's Sweet Chocolate Cake

1 package (4-ounce) German's sweet chocolate
½ cup boiling water
¾ cup shortening, butter, or margarine*
1¾ cups sugar
4 eggs
1 teaspoon vanilla
2¾ cups sifted cake flour
1 teaspoon baking soda
1 teaspoon salt
1 cup buttermilk*
Coconut Pecan Frosting

Melt chocolate in ½ cup boiling water. Cool. Cream butter. Gradually add sugar; continue creaming until light and fluffy. Add eggs, one at a time, beating well after each addition. Blend in vanilla and melted chocolate. Sift flour with soda and salt. Alternately add flour mixture and buttermilk to chocolate mixture, beating after each addition until smooth.

Pour into three 9-inch layer pans that have been lined on bottoms with paper. Bake at 375 degrees F. for 30 to 35 minutes, or until cake tester inserted into center of each layer comes out clean. Cool cake in pans 10 minutes. Remove from pans and finish cooling on racks. Peel off paper. Spread Coconut Pecan Frosting between layers and over top of cake.

Note: For altitudes below 3,000 feet, use 2 cups sugar. For altitudes 5,000 to 7,000 feet, use 1½ cups sugar.

With vegetable shortening, use 1 cup plus 2 tablespoons buttermilk.

Coconut Pecan Frosting

3 egg yolks
1 cup sugar
1 cup evaporated milk
½ cup butter or margarine
1 teaspoon vanilla
1⅓ cups flaked coconut
1 cup chopped pecans

Combine egg yolks, sugar, milk, butter, and vanilla. Cook and stir over medium heat until thickened, 12 to 15 minutes. Add coconut and pecans. Beat until thick enough to spread. Makes 3 cups, enough to cover tops of three 8- or 9-inch layers or one 9x13x2-inch cake.

Chocolate Sheet Cake

½ cup butter or margarine, softened
½ cup shortening, softened
4 tablespoons cocoa
1 cup water
2 cups flour
2 cups sugar
½ cup buttermilk
1 teaspoon baking soda
1 teaspoon cinnamon
1 teaspoon vanilla
2 eggs, beaten
Dash salt

Mix together butter, shortening, cocoa, and water; bring to boil. Pour over flour and sugar, which have been sifted together. Mix well. Add buttermilk, soda, cinnamon, vanilla, eggs, and salt and mix well. Bake 20 minutes at 400 degrees F. in greased and floured jelly roll pan (10x15-inch). Five minutes before cake is done, prepare frosting.

Frosting

½ cup butter or margarine
4 tablespoons cocoa
1 teaspoon vanilla
6 tablespoons milk
4 cups powdered sugar
1 cup chopped nuts

Melt butter; add cocoa, vanilla, and milk, and bring to a boil. Remove from heat and add powdered sugar and nuts. Mix well. Frost cake while hot.

Chocolate Cream Cake

1 baked layer of chocolate cake
2 cups nondairy whipping blend, whipped until stiff
1 recipe chocolate frosting

Split cake layer horizontally. Spread bottom half with whipped topping to within ½ inch of edge. (Topping layer will be about 2 inches thick.) Carefully replace top half of cake. Frost top and sides with chocolate frosting. Sprinkle top with chopped nuts. Keep refrigerated until ready to serve.

Chocolate Frosting

4 tablespoons cocoa
3 cups powdered sugar
4 tablespoons soft butter or margarine
2 or 3 tablespoons milk
1 teaspoon vanilla

Mix cocoa and powdered sugar in mixing bowl. Add softened butter, milk, and vanilla. Beat until smooth.

Quick German Chocolate Cake

1 package white or yellow cake mix*
1 package (3 ounces) instant chocolate pudding mix*
¼ cup flour
2 cups milk
3 egg whites, beaten stiff

Combine first four ingredients and beat according to cake package directions. Fold in egg whites. Spoon into 9x13x2-inch pan. Bake at 375 degrees F. for 35 to 40 minutes, or until cake tests done.

*A cake mix that already contains pudding mix may be used. Prepare according to package directions.

Bienenstich Cake and Chocolate Cream Cake

Black Devil's Food Cake

⅓ cup shortening
1½ cups sugar
3 eggs, well beaten
⅔ cup cocoa
½ cup hot water
2 cups unsifted flour
½ teaspoon salt
1 teaspoon baking soda
1 cup thick sour cream
1 teaspoon vanilla

Cream well the shortening and sugar. Add eggs. Beat cocoa in the hot water until smooth. Add to the creamed mixture. Sift dry ingredients together. Add to the sugar mixture alternately with the sour cream. Add vanilla and beat the mixture well. Bake in three 8-inch or two 9-inch greased and floured layer pans, in a 350 degree F. oven for 20 to 30 minutes or until cake tests done. Remove cake from oven to wire racks. Let cool 10 minutes. Turn from pans and cool on wire rack. Frost with any desired frosting. (For high altitude adjustments, see chart at the end of this section.)

Angel Food Cake

1 cup plus 2 tablespoons sifted cake flour
1½ cups sifted sugar
1¼ cups (10 to 12) egg whites (at room temperature)
¼ teaspoon salt
1¼ teaspoons cream of tartar
1 teaspoon vanilla
¼ teaspoon almond extract

Sift flour and ½ cup sugar together. Combine egg whites, salt, cream of tartar, and flavorings in large bowl. Beat with flat wire whip, sturdy egg beater, or at high speed of electric mixer until soft peaks form. Add remaining 1 cup sugar gradually, ¼ cup at a time, beating well after each addition. When beating by hand, beat 25 strokes after each addition. Sift

in flour mixture in four additions, folding in with 15 fold-over strokes each time and turning bowl frequently. (Do not stir or beat.) After last addition, use 10 to 20 extra folding strokes.

Pour batter into ungreased 9- or 10-inch tube pan. Bake in 375-degree F. oven 35 to 40 minutes for 9-inch cake and 30 to 35 minutes for 10-inch cake, or until cake springs back when pressed lightly. Cool cake in pan, upside down, 1 to 2 hours. Then loosen from sides and center tube with knife and gently pull out cake. (An angel cake pan with a removable bottom is ideal for removing cake in perfect condition.) (For high altitude adjustments, see chart at the end of this section.)

Whipped Cream Valentine Cake

1 10-inch angel food cake, baked and cooled
1 package (10 ounces) frozen strawberries or raspberries, thawed
1 tablespoon (1 envelope) unflavored gelatin
2 cups heavy cream, whipped until stiff
4 tablespoons sugar
1 teaspoon vanilla

Cut angel food cake into 3 horizontal layers. Drain juice off thawed strawberries or raspberries into a small bowl. Over the juice sprinkle gelatin and allow to stand until softened. Set small bowl into hot water and stir until gelatin dissolves.

Combine the gelatin mixture with berries and barely cool. (If it cools too much the gelatin will set.) Add sugar and vanilla to whipped cream. Fold berries into cream. Do not worry if fruit seems too juicy—it will soon set up. Cover the cake layers generously with cream mixture. Adjust the top layer and spread mixture over the entire top and sides of cake. Refrigerate until firm. Makes 10 to 12 servings.

Peppermint Angel Food Dessert

¾ cup crushed red and white peppermint stick
    candy
½ cup milk
1½ teaspoons unflavored gelatin (½ envelope)
2 teaspoons water
1 pint whipping cream, whipped until stiff
1 angel food cake, sliced into 3 horizontal layers
½ cup chocolate syrup

Put candy in milk; heat and stir until dissolved. Soften gelatin in water and add to milk and candy mixture. Chill until it starts to set. Fold into whipped cream. Spread cream mixture over bottom layer of cake. Drizzle chocolate syrup over whipped cream mixture. Place another layer of cake and repeat. Repeat with third layer. Cover outside of cake with whipped cream mixture. Chill and serve. Makes 12 servings.

Strawberry Delight

1 package (3 ounces) strawberry gelatin
1 package (10 ounces) sliced frozen strawberries
1 tablespoon sugar
Dash of salt
1 cup whipping cream, whipped with 1
   tablespoon sugar
½ of a large angel food cake, torn in pieces

Dissolve gelatin in 1¼ cups boiling water. Stir in strawberries, sugar, and salt. Cool until gelatin becomes thick and syrupy. Fold in whipped cream (save about ¼ cup for garnish). Break about one-half of the half cake into a 2- or 3-quart serving bowl. Pour half of the strawberry cream mixture over cake. Add another layer of torn cake pieces and then remaining strawberry cream mixture. Top each serving with a dollop of whipped cream. Makes about 10 servings.

Angel Fluff

1 small (9-ounce) angel cake
1 cup whipping cream, stiffly beaten
1 cup half-and-half cream
1 cup sugar
⅓ cup lemon juice

In your prettiest large serving bowl (2-quart) break cake into bite-size pieces. In small bowl of electric mixer or with hand electric mixer, gradually beat half-and-half into whipped cream. The result will be a fluffy, thick liquid. Beat sugar into cream mixture, adding it gradually, then add lemon juice slowly, still beating. Pour this mixture over cake pieces. Chill for at least 2 hours. Spoon onto dessert plates and serve with pineapple sauce (below). Makes 8 servings.

Pineapple Sauce

4 tablespoons cornstarch
1 cup sugar
2 cups pineapple juice
½ cup lemon juice

Combine cornstarch and sugar and mix well in a small saucepan. Add pineapple juice and cook on medium heat, stirring constantly, until clear and thickened, about 5 minutes. Add lemon juice. Remove from heat. Chill.

Chiffon Cake

1¼ cups sugar
3 teaspoons baking powder
2¼ cups cake flour
1 teaspoon salt
½ cup salad oil
5 egg yolks
¾ cup water
2 teaspoons vanilla
2 teaspoons grated lemon rind (optional)
1 cup egg whites (7 to 8 large)
½ teaspoon cream of tartar

Sift dry ingredients together in a mixing bowl. Add oil, egg yolks, water, vanilla, and lemon rind to the dry ingredients. Beat until smooth. Beat egg whites with cream of tartar until stiff. Pour yolk mixture over whipped whites, folding together until blended. Bake in ungreased 10-inch tube pan at 325 degrees F. for 55 minutes, then at 350 degrees F. for 10 to 15 minutes. When cake tests done, invert tube pan and let hang until cool. (For high altitude adjustments, see chart at the end of this section.)

Orange Sponge Cake

    8 eggs, separated
    ¼ teaspoon salt
    1 teaspoon cream of tartar
    1⅓ cups sugar
    Grated rind from one orange
    ¼ cup orange juice
    1 cup plus 2 tablespoons flour, sifted
    ½ cup almonds, blanched and toasted
    1 cup cream, whipped

Beat egg whites and salt until foamy; add cream of tartar and beat until stiff, not dry. Add ⅔ cup sugar gradually, beating after each addition. Beat egg yolks until very thick and lemon colored; add remaining ⅔ cup sugar, orange rind, and juice. Fold the two mixtures together and fold in flour. Bake for one hour in an ungreased 10-inch angel cake pan at 325 degrees F. Remove from oven and invert for one hour.

Put almonds through food chopper (or chop coarsely). Spread whipped cream on cake and sprinkle with almonds, or glaze with Orange Butter Glaze (see index).

Caramel Pudding Cake

Mix and boil together 4 cups water, 2 cups brown sugar, and 4 tablespoons butter or margarine. Set aside. Prepare batter:

    ¼ cup butter or margarine
    1 cup sugar
    1 cup chopped peeled apples
    2 cups flour
    1 teaspoon nutmeg
    1 teaspoon cinnamon
    2½ teaspoons baking powder
    ½ teaspoon salt
    1½ teaspoons baking soda
    1 cup milk
    1 teaspoon vanilla
    1 cup raisins
    ½ cup chopped nuts
    Whipped topping (optional)

Cream butter; add sugar, and cream together thoroughly. Add chopped apples. Sift dry ingredients together and add alternately with milk. Stir in remaining ingredients. Spread batter into a greased 13x9x2-inch pan. Pour hot brown sugar and butter mixture over batter. Bake at 375 degrees F. for 45 minutes. Cut in squares and serve, warm or cold, with whipped topping, if desired. Makes 20 to 24 servings. *Put a Cookie Sheet Under The 13 x 9 Pan. It will boil over.*

Lemon Bars

    ½ cup soft butter or margarine
    ¼ cup powdered sugar
    1 cup flour

Cream butter and sugar; add flour. Spread in an 8x8-inch pan and bake at 325 degrees F. for 15 to 20 minutes. While crust is baking, prepare next layer:

    2 eggs
    1 cup sugar
    2 tablespoons flour
    2 tablespoons lemon juice
    Grated rind of ½ lemon

Beat eggs slightly and add sugar, flour, lemon juice, and rind. Mix well and pour over hot crust after it comes from oven. Now bake for 15 to 20 minutes at 325 degrees F. Remove from oven and sprinkle with sifted powdered sugar. Cool slightly before cutting into finger cookies. This recipe, when doubled, fits just right into a jelly roll pan (10x15-inch). Good served with vanilla ice cream.

Easy Petits Fours

1 package cake mix, any flavor desired
Frosting or glaze (see below)

Prepare cake batter according to package directions. Bake in a jelly roll pan (15x10x1-inch) that has been lined with wax paper. Use a 350-degree F. oven and bake about 25 minutes, or until cake tests done. Turn cake onto wire racks to cool. Remove paper and trim off edges. Brush off the crumbs so frosting will be smooth. Spread frosting. When frosting has set, mark off long side of cake at about 1½-inch intervals. Mark short side at 2-inch intervals. With a sharp knife, cut cake lengthwise into 5 long strips; now cut crosswise from marked points to make small rectangles, diamonds, or triangles. Decorate if desired. Makes about 50 petits fours.

Note: Petits fours may also be iced on all sides. Cut cake into various-shaped pieces before icing. Then place pieces on a wire rack placed over a piece of waxed paper or baking pan. Pour icing over cake, drizzling down sides as well as top of each piece. Icing that collects on waxed paper or baking pan may be reheated and used if there are no crumbs in it.

Liquid Icing for Petits Fours

3 cups granulated sugar
¼ teaspoon cream of tartar
1½ cups hot water
1 teaspoon vanilla
2½ cups powdered sugar

Put granulated sugar, cream of tartar, and hot water in a 2-quart saucepan. Cover until mixture comes to a boil in order to dissolve sugar crystals. Bring to a boil and cook, uncovered, to a temperature of 226 degrees F. Cool at room temperature to 110 degrees F. (lukewarm). Add vanilla and powdered sugar until of pouring consistency. Beat until smooth. Use to glaze petits fours.

Cheesecake

Crust

1½ cups graham cracker crumbs, rolled fine
3 tablespoons sugar
6 tablespoons butter or margarine
1 teaspoon cinnamon

Thoroughly mix ingredients. Press firmly into a 9- or 10-inch pie pan, lining bottom and sides; set aside. Make filling.

Filling

1½ pounds (3 8-ounce packages) softened cream cheese
1 cup sugar
3 eggs
¾ teaspoon vanilla

Beat cream cheese well. Add sugar a little at a time; add eggs one at a time; add vanilla. Combine thoroughly. Pour into crust; fill to within ½ inch of top to allow room for topping. Bake 60 minutes at 300 degrees F.

Topping

1 pint sour cream
3 tablespoons sugar
½ teaspoon vanilla

Whip sour cream; add sugar gradually; add vanilla. Pour over pie and return to oven. Bake for 10 minutes at 300 degrees F. Cool.

Easy Cherry Cheesecake

2 cups graham cracker crumbs
½ cup melted margarine or butter
1 package (8 ounces) softened cream cheese
2 tablespoons milk
1 cup powdered sugar
½ teaspoon vanilla
2 cups whipped topping (1 envelope mix
    prepared by package directions)
1 can cherry pie filling, or make your own from a
    16-ounce can pie cherries

In a 9x13x2-inch pan, mix graham cracker crumbs with melted margarine. Use a fork and level well, then press firmly in bottom of pan. Combine and mix until smooth the cream cheese, milk, powdered sugar, and vanilla. Fold in the whipped topping. Spread over cracker crumbs. Then cover with chilled cherry pie filling. Chill 2 hours. Makes 18 to 24 servings.

Whole Wheat Crumb Cake

Cake

1½ cups whole wheat flour
¾ cup granulated sugar
¾ cup brown sugar
½ cup shortening
¾ cup chopped dates
¾ cup walnuts, chopped
½ teaspoon salt
¼ teaspoon nutmeg
2 eggs
¾ cup milk
1 teaspoon vanilla
1 teaspoon baking soda

Topping

½ cup white sugar
½ cup brown sugar
½ cup chopped nuts

Cake: Mix flour, sugars, shortening, dates, walnuts, salt, and nutmeg by hand until well blended (do not use electric mixer). Beat eggs; add milk, vanilla, and baking soda. Add liquid ingredients to dry ingredients. Stir just a few times until dry ingredients are moistened. Pour into a well-greased 9x12-inch pan.

Topping: Mix sugars and chopped nuts together with fingers until blended. Sprinkle over top of batter.

Bake at 350 degrees F. for 25 minutes. This cake is delicious served warm just plain, or you may serve with whipped cream, ice cream, or a caramel, lemon, or vanilla sauce.

Coconut Brunch Cake

4 eggs
2 cups sugar
1 cup salad oil
3 cups flour
½ teaspoon baking soda
½ teaspoon baking powder
½ teaspoon salt
1 cup buttermilk
2 teaspoons coconut flavoring
1 cup coconut
1 cup walnuts, chopped

In large mixing bowl, beat eggs, sugar, and salad oil. Sift flour, baking soda, baking powder, and salt. Add dry ingredients to creamed mixture alternately with buttermilk. Add coconut flavoring, coconut, and walnuts. Generously grease and flour a 10-inch Bundt pan. Pour batter into pan. Bake at 350 degrees F. for 1 hour.

Meanwhile, mix in a saucepan 1 cup sugar, ½ cup water, and 3 tablespoons butter or margarine. Bring to boil and cook for 5 minutes. When cake is done, leave in pan and pour hot syrup over top of cake. Allow to stand for 4 hours; then remove from pan.

Gingerbread

½ cup sugar
½ cup butter or margarine
1 egg, well beaten
1 cup molasses
½ teaspoon salt
2½ cups sifted flour
1½ teaspoons baking soda
1 teaspoon cinnamon
1 teaspoon ginger
½ teaspoon powdered cloves
1 cup very hot water
Bananas
Whipped cream

Cream sugar and butter well. Add eggs and molasses. Beat well. Sift dry ingredients together and add to creamed mixture. Add hot water and beat until smooth (batter will be very thin). Pour into a well-greased 9x13-inch baking pan. Bake in a 350-degree oven for about 40 minutes, or until cake tests done. Serve warm or cold with sliced bananas and whipped cream.

Poppy Seed Cake

1 package (18-ounce) yellow cake mix
1 package (3¾ ounces) <u>instant</u> French vanilla
   pudding mix
4 eggs
1 cup thick sour cream
½ cup water
1 teaspoon rum flavoring
½ cup butter or margarine, melted (or use
   butter-flavored oil)
¼ cup poppy seeds

Combine cake and pudding mixes, eggs, sour cream, water, rum flavoring, butter, and poppy seeds in large bowl of electric mixer. Blend well on low speed, then beat at medium speed for 5 minutes.

Pour batter into well-greased and lightly floured Bundt cake pan. Bake at 350 degrees F. for about 45 minutes, or until cake tests done.

Remove from oven and cool in pan for 15 minutes. Turn out onto cake rack and cool completely. Sift a light dusting of powdered sugar over cake, if desired.

This delicious cake dessert is also good sliced thin and served as a bread with fruit salad.

Spritz Cookies

½ cup butter, softened
⅓ cup sugar
¼ teaspoon vanilla or almond extract
1 egg yolk
1¼ cups flour

Cream together butter and sugar. Add flavoring and egg yolk. Mix in flour gradually. Put dough into cookie press and force into desired shapes onto an ungreased baking sheet. Decorate with maraschino cherry half if desired. Bake at 375 degrees F. for 7 to 10 minutes. Remove cookies immediately from baking pan to wire racks. Makes 2 dozen cookies.

Cherry Macaroons

1½ cups sugar
1⅓ cups shortening
2 eggs, unbeaten
3½ cups flour
2 teaspoons baking powder
2 teaspoons baking soda
½ teaspoon salt
¾ cup maraschino cherries, drained and
   chopped
1½ teaspoons almond extract
1 cup coconut

Cream sugar and shortening. Add eggs and beat until fluffy. Sift flour, baking powder, baking soda, and salt and add to creamed mixture. Add maraschino cherries, almond extract, and coconut and mix well. Drop by teaspoonfuls onto greased cookie sheet. Bake at 350 degrees F. for 10 to 12 minutes.

Oatmeal Cookies

2 cups brown sugar
1 cup shortening
2 eggs
¼ cup milk
2 cups quick rolled oats
½ teaspoon salt
1 teaspoon baking soda
1 teaspoon allspice
1 teaspoon cinnamon
1 teaspoon cloves
1 teaspoon nutmeg
2 cups flour
1 cup raisins
½ cup nuts

Cream together sugar and shortening. Add eggs and milk and mix well. Then add rolled oats. Sift together dry ingredients and mix in until smooth. Stir in raisins and nuts. Drop on cookie sheet and bake at 375 degrees F. for 10 minutes or until lightly browned. Makes 5 to 6 dozen cookies.

Sugar Cookies

1½ cups sugar
⅔ cup shortening or butter
2 eggs, beaten
2 tablespoons milk
1 teaspoon vanilla
3¼ cups flour
2½ teaspoons baking powder
½ teaspoon salt
Decorative toppings, below (optional)

Cream sugar and shortening (butter makes a better-tasting cookie). Add eggs, milk, and vanilla. Sift dry ingredients together and beat into creamed mixture, combining thoroughly. With hands, shape dough into a ball; wrap and refrigerate 2 to 3 hours (or overnight) until easy to handle.

Grease cookie sheets lightly. On lightly floured board, roll one-half or one-third of the dough at one time, keeping the rest refrigerated. For crisp cookies, roll dough paper-thin. For softer cookies, roll ⅛-inch to ¼-inch thick. Cut into shapes desired with a floured cookie cutter. Reroll trimmings and cut.

Place cookies one-half inch apart on cookie sheets. Sprinkle with decorative toppings. Bake at 400 degrees F. about 8 minutes or until a very light brown. Remove cookies to racks to cool. Makes about 6 dozen cookies.

Decorative Toppings: Brush cookies with heavy cream or with a mixture of one egg white slightly beaten with one tablespoon water; sprinkle with sugar, nonpareils, chopped nuts, shredded coconut, cut-up gumdrops, or butterscotch pieces.

Iced Carrot Cookies

1 cup shortening
¾ cup sugar
2 eggs
1 cup cooked, mashed carrots
2 cups flour
2 teaspoons baking powder
½ teaspoon salt
¾ cup coconut

Cream shortening and sugar in a large mixing bowl. Add eggs and beat until fluffy. Add mashed carrots. Sift flour, baking powder, and salt, and add to creamed mixture. Stir in coconut. Drop by teaspoonfuls onto a greased cookie sheet. Bake at 400 degrees F. for 10 minutes. Cool, then ice with Orange Frosting (below). Makes 4 dozen small cookies.

Orange Frosting

In a small bowl, combine 1 tablespoon orange juice, 2 teaspoons grated orange peel, 1 cup powdered sugar, and 2 tablespoons soft margarine; stir until well mixed.

Gingerbread with Whipped Cream and Bananas

Scotch Shortbread

2 cups (1 pound) butter, softened
1 cup sugar
4 cups flour

Cream butter and add sugar. Beat until light and fluffy. Add flour and mix well. Chill several hours. Roll out about ¼-inch thick on a floured board. Cut into 2x2-inch squares and place on an ungreased baking sheet. Prick each cookie several times with a fork. Bake at 325 degrees F. about 30 minutes, until cookies are delicately brown. Cool slightly before removing from cookie sheet. Makes about 40 cookies.

Old-Fashioned Filled Cookies

½ cup butter or margarine
¾ cup sugar
1 egg
2¼ cups flour
2 teaspoons baking powder
½ teaspoon salt
¼ teaspoon nutmeg
2 tablespoons milk
½ teaspoon vanilla

Cream butter. Add sugar and egg, and beat until fluffy. Sift flour, baking powder, salt, and nutmeg. Add to creamed mixture alternately with milk. Add vanilla. Chill dough for one hour in refrigerator. Prepare raisin filling (below).

Roll dough out to ¼ inch thick. Cut with a round cookie cutter approximately 3 inches in diameter. Cut 2 rounds for each cookie. Place about 1 teaspoon raisin filling in center of a round, and top with a second round. Press edges together with fingers or a fork. Prick top with fork. Place on a greased cookie sheet and bake at 350 degrees F. for 10 minutes or until just done.

Raisin Filling

1 cup ground raisins
¼ cup water
¼ cup sugar
¼ cup chopped nuts
1 teaspoon lemon juice

Place all ingredients in a small saucepan and cook on low heat until thick, stirring constantly. Cool.

Layered Cookies

¼ pound butter or margarine
1 cup graham cracker crumbs
1 cup coconut
1 cup chocolate chips
1 cup butterscotch chips
1 cup chopped nuts
1 can sweetened condensed milk

Melt butter in a 9x13-inch pan. Sprinkle over the butter, in layers, the remaining ingredients. Bake at 350 degrees F. for 30 minutes. Cut away from sides of pan when you take from oven. Cut in squares while still warm.

Orange Butter Glaze

1½ tablespoons milk
1 tablespoon butter
1¼ cups powdered sugar
1 tablespoon orange juice
½ teaspoon grated orange rind

Heat milk and butter together. Stir in sugar and mix until smooth. Add orange juice and rind. Beat until shiny. Add a drop or two more liquid if needed to make desired spreading consistency. Makes about ½ cup, or enough to glaze top of 10-inch tube cake, an 8- or 9-inch-square cake, or a 9x5x3-inch loaf.

Lemon Butter Glaze: Prepare as for Orange Butter Glaze, substituting lemon juice and rind for the orange juice and rind.

Chocolate Frosting

¼ cup butter or margarine, melted
½ cup cocoa (not a mix)
¼ teaspoon salt
Milk (about ⅓ cup)
1½ teaspoons vanilla
3½ to 4 cups powdered sugar

In saucepan, melt butter. Remove from heat and add cocoa and salt. Stir in milk and vanilla. Add this mixture to the sugar in a mixing bowl. Mix or beat until smooth and of proper spreading consistency.

Amounts of Frosting to Use

The following chart suggests the ideal amount of butter cream or fudge-type frosting for various sized cakes. In all cases, about twice as much of the fluffy-type frostings, such as Seven Minute and Sea Foam, should be used.

	Center	Sides	Top	Total
8-inch layer cake	½ cup	1 cup	¾ cup	2¼ cups
9-inch layer cake	⅔ cup	1¼ cups	¾ cup	2⅔ cups
8-inch square cake		⅔ cup	⅔ cup	1⅓ cups
9-inch square cake		1 cup	1 cup	2 cups
13x9-inch cake		1 cup	1⅓ cups	2⅓ cups
24 cupcakes				2¼ cups
10-inch tube cake		1½ cups	¾ cup	2¼ cups

Recipe Adjustments for Baking at Higher Altitudes

Most cake recipes for sea level need no modification up to the altitude of 2,500 or 3,000 feet. Above that it is often necessary to adjust recipes slightly in proportions of certain ingredients. Usually, a decrease in leavening or sugar (or both) and an increase in liquid are needed.

Each or all of these adjustments may be required to a greater or lesser degree, for every recipe is different in richness and in its balance of ingredients. Only *repeated experiments* with each recipe can give the most successful proportions to use.

The table below is a helpful starting point or guide. It may be all that is needed to adjust a sea level recipe to your altitude.

Cake Recipe Adjustment Guide for High Altitudes*

Adjustment	4,000 to 5,000 feet	5,000 to 7,000 feet
Reduce baking powder For each teaspoon, decrease	⅛ to ¼ teaspoon	¼ teaspoon
Reduce sugar For each cup, decrease	0 to 2 tablespoons	1 to 3 tablespoons
Increase liquid For each cup, add	2 to 4 tablespoons	3 to 4 tablespoons

Note: When two amounts are given, the smaller adjustment should be tried first; then if the cake still needs improvement, the larger adjustment can be used the next time.

In making very rich cakes at high altitudes, it is sometimes necessary to reduce shortening by 1 or 2 tablespoons. Recipes using baking soda may require a very slight reduction of this leavening. On the other hand, the amount of egg may be increased at highest altitudes. This has possibilities in recipe adjustments for angel food and sponge cakes.

Most cake mixes give special adjustment for high altitude on the package.

Pies and Pastries

Lion House Pie Dough

¼ cup butter
¼ cup margarine
⅓ cup vegetable shortening
⅓ cup lard
1 tablespoon sugar
½ teaspoon baking powder
1 teaspoon salt
1 tablespoon nonfat dry milk
3 cups unsifted all-purpose flour
½ cup cold water (may need 1 tablespoon more water)

In a mixer cream together the fats. Add sugar, baking powder, salt, and dry milk. Add half the flour and mix well. Add water and remaining flour. This can all be done in the mixer. (This crust can also be made using the traditional pie crust method, by hand-cutting fat into dry ingredients.)

Roll out half of the pastry very thin. Line a pie pan. Trim pastry ¼ inch beyond rim of pie pan. Roll out remaining pastry for top crust. Cut several slits or a fancy design near center. Fill bottom crust. Moisten the edge of the bottom crust and center top crust over filling. Open slits with knife (steam must escape during baking). Trim the top crust, letting it extend ½ inch over rim. To seal, press top and bottom crusts together on rim. Then fold edge of top crust under bottom crust and flute. Bake according to directions in individual recipe.

Makes one 9-inch two-crust pie. This is a very pliable, tender, easy-to-handle dough. If you are making an 8-inch pie, extra dough may be wrapped well in plastic wrap and stored in the freezer for future use. Leftover pie dough makes excellent tarts.

Blueberry Pie

¼ cup quick-cooking tapioca
¼ cup sugar
2 tablespoons brown sugar
¼ teaspoon salt
⅛ teaspoon cinnamon
2 packages (about 12 ounces each) frozen sweetened blueberries, thawed and drained (about 2 cups)*
½ cup blueberry juice
1 tablespoon lemon juice
Pastry for 8-inch two-crust pie
1 tablespoon butter or margarine

Combine tapioca, sugars, salt, cinnamon, blueberries, blueberry juice, and lemon juice; set aside. Prepare pastry crusts. Roll out bottom crust and fit snugly into pie pan. Roll out top crust and cut two 2-inch slits near center, then snip with scissors at sides and between slits. Or make any fancy cut-out design desired.

Pour filling into shell. Dot with butter. Moisten edge of bottom crust rim. To adjust top crust, fold in half or roll loosely on rolling pin; center on filling. Pull slits apart slightly if necessary with a knife. (Steam must escape during baking.) Trim top crust, allowing it to extend ½ inch over rim. To seal, press top and bottom crusts together on rim. Then fold edge of top crust under bottom and flute. Bake at 425 degrees F. about 45 minutes, or until syrup boils with heavy bubbles and crust is nicely browned.

*Canned blueberries may be used—2 cans (14 ounces each) blueberries, drained. Reduce tapioca to 3 tablespoons. Add ¼ teaspoon almond extract and grated orange rind to combined fruit mixture.

Apricot-Pineapple Pie

Pastry for 9-inch two-crust pie
1 can (1 lb. 14-ounce) unpeeled apricot halves, drained
1 can (15½-ounce) pineapple chunks, drained
½ cup sugar
2 tablespoons cornstarch
Pinch salt
½ cup juice drained from pineapple

Line pie pan with pastry. Mix sugar, cornstarch, and salt in saucepan. Add juice and cook until thick, stirring constantly. Add fruits, then pour into pie shell. Cover with top crust that has slits cut in it to release steam. Seal edges together and flute. Bake at 400 degrees F. for 45 minutes, or until crust is browned.

Two-Crust Cranberry Pie

2 cups raw cranberries
1 cup water
1 cup sugar
1¾ tablespoons cornstarch
¼ to ½ cup chopped walnuts
2 teaspoons butter or margarine
Pastry for 8-inch two-crust pie

In medium-size saucepan cook cranberries in the water until the skins pop. Strain and save the juice. Combine juice, sugar, and cornstarch. Cook mixture until it thickens and bubbles, stirring constantly. Stir in walnuts, cranberries, and butter. Pour into pie shell; cover with top crust. Bake at 400 degrees F. for 10 minutes. Reduce heat to 350 degrees F. for 45 minutes or until crust is nicely browned.

Boysenberry or Gooseberry Pie*

2 cans (14 ounces each) or 4 cups boysenberries or gooseberries*
½ cup cornstarch
1 cup sugar
¼ teaspoon salt
Pastry for 8-inch two-crust pie

Drain boysenberries and save juice. Mix cornstarch, sugar, and salt together in small saucepan. Add heated juice; cook and stir until thick, about 5 minutes after mixture comes to a full boil, stirring constantly. Remove from heat and cool.

Prepare pastry crusts. Roll out bottom crust and fit it snugly into an 8-inch pie pan. Roll out top crust and cut two 2-inch slits near center, then snip with scissors at sides and between slits. Or make any fancy cut-out design desired.

Pour cooled filling into shell. Moisten edge of bottom crust rim. To adjust top crust, fold in half or roll loosely on rolling pin; center on filling. Pull slits apart slightly, if necessary, with a knife. (Steam must escape during baking.) Trim top crust, allowing it to extend one-half inch over rim. To seal, press top and bottom crusts together on rim. Then fold edge of top crust under bottom and flute. Bake at 400 degrees F. for 45 minutes. Makes one 8-inch pie.

*Blueberry pie can also be made using this recipe and canned blueberries.

Cranberry Pie

2½ cups fresh cranberries
1 cup water
¾ cup raisins
1 cup sugar
4 tablespoons cornstarch
½ cup chopped walnuts
2 tablespoons butter
Baked 9-inch pie shell
Whipped cream

→

In a medium saucepan cook cranberries in 1 cup water until cranberries pop. Add raisins. Combine sugar and cornstarch and stir into cranberry mixture. Cook and stir until mixture thickens and bubbles. Add nuts and butter and stir until butter melts. Pour into pie shell. Cool. Serve with a dollop of whipped cream.

Apple Pie

Pastry for 9-inch two-crust pie
4 to 5 cups tart apples, peeled, cored, and sliced
¼ to ½ cup water
¾ to 1 cup sugar
1 to 2 tablespoons flour
½ to 1 teaspoon cinnamon
⅛ teaspoon salt
1 tablespoon lemon juice
2 tablespoons butter or margarine

Steam or simmer apples gently in water until they wilt and begin to become transparent. (This is a partial cooking only so that apples will cook thoroughly in the pie.)

Combine the sugar and other dry ingredients. Mix well. Spread half over the pastry-lined pie pan. Lift apples from cooking liquid into crust. Add ¼ cup of the cooking liquid. Sprinkle with remaining sugar mixture. Sprinkle pie filling with lemon juice and dot with butter. Roll, fit, and seal top crust. Brush with milk and sprinkle with sugar, if desired.

Bake on lower shelf of oven at 425 degrees F. for 30 to 40 minutes, or until nicely browned.

Note: Apple pie is only as good as the apples it is made with. Tart, juicy apples are desirable, and some judgment is necessary as to amounts of sugar and thickening when sweeter, less juicy apples are used.

Swiss Apple-Cherry Pie

4 tart apples
6 tablespoons butter or margarine
1 cup sugar
2 tablespoons flour
2 teaspoons cinnamon
½ teaspoon nutmeg
1 can (#2½ size) pitted sour red cherries, drained
Pastry for 9-inch two-crust pie

Pare apples; core and slice. Melt 2 tablespoons butter and brush on bottom of pastry shell. Arrange a layer of sliced apples on bottom of shell. Mix dry ingredients and sprinkle about one-fourth over layer of apples. Arrange layer of cherries and sprinkle with one-fourth of dry ingredients—then apples, dry ingredients, then cherries, dry ingredients, and end with layer of apples. Top with dots of remaining butter. After top crust is placed on pie, brush crust with cream or evaporated milk and sprinkle ½ teaspoon sugar mixed with ¼ teaspoon cinnamon over top. Cut vents in top crust. Bake at 425 degrees F. for 30 to 40 minutes. Serve with a scoop of vanilla ice cream.

Rhubarb Pie

1⅓ cups sugar
2 tablespoons flour
1 egg
3 cups fresh or frozen rhubarb, cut in 1-inch pieces
3 drops red food coloring
Pastry for 9-inch two-crust pie

Combine sugar and flour. Beat egg and blend with the flour mixture. Add rhubarb and red food coloring. Mix well. Pour into unbaked 9-inch pie shell. Roll out top crust; cut slits and place over filling. Seal, then flute edges. Brush top with milk and sprinkle with sugar, if desired. Bake at 400 degrees F. for 45 minutes or until nicely browned.

Apple Pie with Cheese

Cherry Pie

2½ tablespoons quick-cooking tapioca
⅛ teaspoon salt
1 cup sugar
6 drops red food coloring
3 cups drained water-packed red sour
   cherries
½ cup cherry juice
¼ teaspoon almond extract
Pastry for 9-inch two-crust pie
1 tablespoon butter

Combine all ingredients except pastry and butter. Let stand about 15 minutes. Pour into pie shell; dot filling with butter. Cut air vents in top crust and place over filling; press top and bottom crusts together on edge of pie pan. Crimp or flute. Bake pie at 425 degrees F. for about 50 minutes.

Lemon Cream Pie

1¼ cups sugar
¼ teaspoon salt
6 tablespoons cornstarch
1½ cups boiling water
3 eggs, slightly beaten
6 tablespoons lemon juice
¼ teaspoon grated lemon rind
2 tablespoons butter or margarine
1 cup heavy cream, whipped and sweetened
Baked 9-inch pie shell

Combine sugar, salt, and cornstarch in a 2- or 3-quart saucepan. Blend well. Place over medium heat and add boiling water, stirring rapidly until smooth and thick. Bring to a full boil to thoroughly cook the cornstarch. Remove from heat. Add a little of the hot pudding to the eggs while stirring rapidly. Return egg mixture to hot pudding and reheat, stirring constantly, just until smooth.

Remove from heat and add lemon juice and rind and butter. Pour filling into baked pie shell. Chill. Serve topped with whipped cream.

LEMON MERINGUE PIE: Make as above except separate the eggs, using only the yolks in the filling. Beat the whites on high speed of the electric mixer, adding 6 tablespoons of sugar gradually while beating. Continue beating until mixture stands in stiff peaks. Pile on hot filling; seal well to edge of pie crust. Bake at 375 degrees F. for about 15 minutes, or until delicately browned. Cool thoroughly, at least 4 hours.

Lemonade Chiffon Pie

1 envelope (1 tablespoon) unflavored gelatin
¼ cup cold water
½ cup boiling water
⅔ cup sugar
1 can (6 ounces) frozen lemonade concentrate
1 cup heavy cream, whipped
Baked 9-inch pie shell

Mix gelatin and cold water together. Add boiling water and sugar; stir until dissolved. Add lemonade concentrate; stir until dissolved. Chill until very thick. Fold whipped cream into chilled mixture. Pour into pie shell. Chill. Serve with additional whipped cream, if desired.

Fresh Strawberry Pie

1½ quarts fresh strawberries
1 cup sugar
3 tablespoons cornstarch
2 tablespoons lemon juice
1 cup whipping cream
Baked 9-inch pie shell

Wash berries and remove caps. Reserve about half the berries, the largest and best-colored ones. Mash the rest of the berries. Add the sugar and cornstarch that have been mixed together. Place over medium heat and cook until smooth and thick, stirring constantly. Stir in lemon juice. Cool.   ↗

Add the whole berries to the cooled mixture, saving a few for garnish, if desired. Pour into pie shell. Chill until set. When ready to serve, whip the cream and spread over pie. Garnish with whole berries. Makes 6 servings.

Raisin Pie

1½ cups raisins
1½ cups water
¼ cup pineapple juice (or use ¼ cup more water)
½ teaspoon vanilla
1 cup sugar
¼ cup cornstarch
½ teaspoon salt
¼ cup lemon juice
Pastry for 8-inch two-crust pie (rolled thin)

In a small saucepan combine raisins, water, pineapple juice, and vanilla. Bring to a boil and cook 5 minutes. Pour mixture through strainer. Set raisins aside and reserve the liquid.

Mix together sugar, cornstarch, and salt; add hot raisin liquid, beating all together with a wire whip. Continue cooking and stirring until thick, about 5 minutes. Add raisins and lemon juice and pour into unbaked pie shell.

Roll out top crust and cut two 2-inch slits near center, then snip with scissors at sides and between slits. Or make any fancy cut-out design desired. Moisten edge of bottom crust rim. To adjust top crust, fold in half or roll loosely on rolling pin; center on filling. Pull slits apart slightly if necessary with a knife. (Steam must escape during baking.) Trim top crust, allowing it to extend ½ inch over rim. To seal, press top and bottom crusts together on rim. Then fold edge of top crust under bottom and flute. Bake at 400 degrees F. for about 45 minutes or to the desired brownness.

Butterscotch Cream Pie

1⅓ cups sugar
2½ cups milk
¾ cup table cream
5 tablespoons cornstarch
¼ teaspoon salt
3 egg yolks*
1 teaspoon vanilla
2 tablespoons butter or margarine
1 cup whipping cream
¼ cup chopped nuts, if desired
Baked 9-inch pie crust

Measure sugar into a heavy saucepan or skillet. Stir constantly over high heat until sugar is nearly melted. Reduce heat to medium and continue stirring until all sugar is melted and a light amber color. In the meantime, heat milk; stir hot milk into melted sugar cautiously. Sugar will bubble and steam, then harden. Keep heat on low and stir occasionally until the hard sugar completely dissolves in the milk.

Add the table cream to the cornstarch gradually to make a smooth paste, then stir into hot milk mixture; cook and stir until a smooth, thick pudding is formed. Let it boil a minute or two, stirring vigorously, then remove from heat. Add salt to egg yolks, then stir in some of the hot pudding. Stir the egg mixture back into the pudding and cook another 2 to 3 minutes. Remove from heat. Add vanilla and butter. Cool 5 minutes, then pour into baked pie shell. Chill 3 to 4 hours. When ready to serve, whip the cream and spread over pie. Sprinkle with nuts. Makes 6 servings.

*2 whole eggs may be used, but filling may not be as smooth.

Four-Step Black Bottom Pie

Crush 36 gingersnaps; roll fine and combine with ½ cup melted butter or margarine and a dash of salt. Mold evenly into an 11-inch springform pan. Prepare filling:

> 4 cups milk
> 4 tablespoons butter or margarine
> ½ cup cornstarch
> 1½ cups sugar
> 4 egg yolks, slightly beaten
> 2 teaspoons vanilla
> 2 squares baking chocolate
> 2 envelopes (2 tablespoons) unflavored gelatin
> ½ cup cold water
> 4 egg whites, beaten stiff
> 1 cup sugar
> 1 teaspoon cream of tartar
> 2 teaspoons imitation rum flavoring
> 1 cup whipped cream, sweetened if desired

Step 1: Scald milk; add butter. Combine cornstarch and sugar; moisten with enough water to make paste. Stir paste into scalded milk and cook until mixture comes to a boil, stirring constantly. Stir hot mixture gradually into slighty beaten egg yolks. Return to heat and cook 2 minutes. Add vanilla. Remove 2 cups of custard. Add chocolate to the custard and beat well. Pour into the crumb crust and chill.

Step 2: Blend gelatin with cold water. Let it swell a few minutes, then fold into the remaining hot custard; let cool.

Step 3: Beat egg whites, 1 cup of sugar, and cream of tartar into a meringue. Add rum flavoring and fold into step 2 custard.

Step 4: As soon as the chocolate custard has set, pour plain custard on top and chill until set. Serve with whipped cream and bits of chocolate for decoration.

Coconut Custard Pie

> 1¼ cups milk
> ½ cup half-and-half cream
> ¼ cup sugar
> ¼ teaspoon nutmeg
> ¼ teaspoon cinnamon
> ¼ teaspoon vanilla
> ⅛ teaspoon salt
> 3 eggs, slightly beaten
> ½ cup flaked coconut
> Unbaked 9-inch pie shell

Combine all ingredients except coconut. Blend well. Cook on low heat or in double boiler until the mixture boils, stirring constantly. Place coconut in pie shell. Pour mixture over coconut until shell is full. Bake at 400 degrees F. for 1 hour, or until knife inserted comes out clean.

Baked Alaska Pie

> 1 8-inch baked pie shell
> 1 quart peppermint ice cream
> 2 to 3 tablespoons chocolate syrup
> 5 egg whites
> 1 teaspoon vanilla
> ½ teaspoon cream of tartar
> ⅔ cup sugar

Spoon ice cream into pie shell. Drizzle with chocolate syrup. Place in freezer until ready to use.

Heat oven to 500 degrees F. Beat egg whites, vanilla, and cream of tartar until foamy. Gradually beat in sugar until mixture is stiff and glossy. Completely cover ice cream in pie shell with meringue, sealing well to edge of crust and piling high. (If desired, pie may be frozen up to 24 hours at this point.) When ready to serve, bake pie on lowest oven rack for 3 to 5 minutes or until meringue is light brown. Serve immediately. Or again return to freezer until ready to serve. Makes 6 to 8 servings.

Basic Cream Pie

 5 tablespoons cornstarch
 1 cup sugar
 ¼ teaspoon salt
 2½ cups milk
 ¾ cup half-and-half cream
 3 egg yolks*
 2 tablespoons butter or margarine
 1 teaspoon vanilla
 1 cup whipping cream
 Baked 9-inch pie shell

Mix cornstarch, sugar, and salt in a 3-quart saucepan. Add milk and cream and cook over medium heat until smooth and thick, stirring constantly. Pour small amount of hot mixture into egg yolks; blend thoroughly, then pour back into saucepan. Cook another 2 or 3 minutes. Remove from heat and add butter and vanilla.

COCONUT CREAM PIE: Add ½ cup coconut (toasted, if desired) to pie filling. Pour into baked shell. Chill 3 to 4 hours. When ready to serve, whip the cream and spread over pie. Top with another ½ cup coconut.

BANANA CREAM PIE: Slice 2 bananas into pie shell. Pour the filling over the bananas. Chill 3 to 4 hours. When ready to serve, whip cream and spread over pie.

CHOCOLATE CREAM PIE: Decrease sugar in pie filling to ¾ cup. Add ½ cup chocolate syrup to cooked mixture. (Or use the full cup of sugar and ½ cup melted chocolate chips.) Pour into pie shell. Chill 3 to 4 hours. When ready to serve, whip cream and spread over pie. Makes 6 servings.

2 whole eggs may be used, but filling may not be as smooth.

Pumpkin Chiffon Pie

 ¼ cup butter, melted
 1¼ cups fine gingersnap crumbs (18 cookies)
 1 envelope (1 tablespoon) unflavored gelatin
 ¼ cup cold water
 ¾ cup brown sugar
 ½ teaspoon salt
 2 teaspoons cinnamon
 ½ teaspoon ginger
 ½ teaspoon allspice
 1⅓ cups mashed, cooked pumpkin
 3 large egg yolks
 ½ cup cold milk

Mix melted butter into gingersnap crumbs. Pat and press into a 9-inch pie pan. Bake at 325 degrees F. for 10 minutes. Cool. Prepare filling: Blend gelatin and cold water. Set aside. Mix together in a saucepan the remaining ingredients. Cook over low heat, stirring until mixture boils. Boil 1 minute; remove from heat. Stir in softened gelatin; cool. When partially set, beat until smooth. Carefully fold in a meringue made from 3 large egg whites, ¼ teaspoon cream of tartar, and 6 tablespoons sugar. Pile into ginger cookie crust. Chill until set (at least 2 hours). Garnish with whipped cream and bits of sugared ginger, if desired.

Puff Pastries

 1 cup flour
 ¼ teaspoon salt
 ½ cup butter (or ¼ cup shortening and ¼ cup butter)
 1 cup boiling water
 4 eggs

Sift flour with salt. Combine fat and boiling water in saucepan; keep on low heat until fat is melted. Add flour all at once and stir vigorously until mixture forms a ball and leaves sides of pan. Cook about 2 minutes until mixture is very dry. Remove from heat. Add unbeaten eggs one at a time and beat well after each addition. Continue beating until a thick dough forms. For cream puffs, drop by tablespoonfuls onto a brown paper-lined baking sheet, about 2 inches apart. (See variations below for other baking directions.) Place in a 425 degree F. oven and bake about 15 minutes. Reduce heat to 400, then to 375 degrees. Bake about 30 to 40 minutes total, or until beads of moisture no longer appear on the surface. Do not open oven door during early part of baking. Remove to wire racks to cool. When cool, cut a slit in side of each puff; remove doughy centers, if necessary. Makes about 12 large cream puff shells.

To Make Cream Puffs: Fill with a cream filling made from a pudding and pie filling mix, following package directions, or fill with sweetened whipped cream or with any other favorite cream filling.

To Make Eclairs: Force dough through a decorating tube onto paper-lined baking sheets in strips about 1-inch wide and 4-inches long. Bake about 25 minutes. Fill as for cream puffs. Frost with chocolate powdered sugar frosting. Makes about 18 eclairs.

To Make Cocktail Puffs: Drop dough by small teaspoonfuls onto paper-lined baking sheets. Bake 17 to 20 minutes. Fill with any savory filling. (See Ribbon Sandwich fillings, for example.) Makes 4 to 5 dozen small puffs.

To Make Puff Shells: Drop dough from tablespoon into deep hot fat (375 degrees F.). Fry 10 to 15 minutes or until a good crust forms, turning often. Drain well, then cut top off each shell. Fill hot shells with creamed fish, poultry, meat, eggs, or vegetables. Or cool the shells and fill with a salad mixture. Replace tops before serving. Makes about 12 large shells.

Pumpkin Pie

2 eggs, slightly beaten
2 cups (1 pound can) pumpkin
¾ cup sugar
½ teaspoon salt
1 teaspoon cinnamon
½ teaspoon ginger
¼ teaspoon cloves
1⅔ cups (13-ounce can) evaporated milk
Unbaked 9-inch pie shell
1 cup whipping cream, whipped (if desired)

Combine ingredients. Mix well. Pour into pie shell. Bake at 425 degrees F. for 15 minutes. Reduce heat to 350 degrees F. and bake an additional 45 minutes. Cool. Serve topped with sweetened whipping cream, if desired.

Chocolate Party Puffs

1 recipe cocktail puffs (make 60 puffs)
1 quart vanilla ice cream
1 quart heavy cream, whipped
1 tablespoon sugar, or to taste
1 teaspoon vanilla, or to taste
1 cup chocolate syrup
1 jar (16 ounces) maraschino cherries, well drained

Slit cooled puffs and pull out any dough strands that may be inside. Fill shells with vanilla ice cream. Freeze on a tray in a single layer. Pack in plastic bags and store in freezer until ready to use.

To assemble, whip the cream; add sugar, vanilla, and syrup. Fold the slightly thawed puffs and cherries into the cream. Serve immediately from a glass bowl. Makes 20 servings of 3 puffs each, 15 servings of 4 puffs each.

Pralines and Cream Pie

1 recipe Basic Cream Pie filling (page 104)
20 individually wrapped caramels
½ cup pecans, chopped
Whipped cream
Whole pecans for garnish

Make cream pie filling. Remove cellophane wrappers from caramels. While filling is still hot, add caramels and chopped pecans. Stir until caramels just start to melt. Pour into baked pie shell. Cool. Top with whipped cream and garnish with whole pecans.

Grasshopper Pie

Chocolate Crust

1 ½ cups finely crushed chocolate
**   wafers (25 wafers)**
6 tablespoons butter or margarine, melted

Filling

6½ cups miniature marshmallows
½ cup milk
¼ cup creme de menthe syrup
1 cup whipping cream
Few drops of green food coloring
**   (optional)**
Chocolate curls for garnish

Prepare crust: Combine the crushed wafers and melted butter. Pour into a 9-inch pie plate. Spread evenly on bottom and sides of pie plate to form a firm, even crust. Chill about 1 hour.

Prepare filling: In a saucepan, combine marshmallows and milk. Cook over low heat until marshmallows are melted. Remove from heat and cool. Stir several times while cooling. Add creme de menthe. Whip cream and fold into marshmallow mixture. Add food coloring, if desired.

Assemble pie: Pour filling into chocolate crust. Garnish with whipped cream and chocolate curls.

Key Lime Pie

2 envelopes unflavored gelatin
1 cup sugar
¼ teaspoon salt
6 egg yolks
¾ cup lime juice
½ cup water
1 teaspoon grated lime peel
Few drops of green food coloring
6 egg whites
¾ cup sugar
2 baked pie shells or graham cracker shells
Whipped cream
Lime, sliced thin for garnish

Mix gelatin, 1 cup sugar, and salt. Beat egg yolks, lime juice, and water and pour into a saucepan. Add gelatin mixture and heat on medium heat until mixture boils, stirring constantly. Stir in lime peel and food coloring. Pour into a bowl, and refrigerate until mixture mounds when dropped from spoon (*do not leave in aluminum pan*). Beat egg whites until soft peaks form. Gradually add ¾ cup sugar and continue beating until stiff. Fold into lime mixture. Pour into pie shells. Serve with whipped cream and garnish with thin slices of lime.

Desserts and Dessert Sauces

Apple Crisp

   1 quart (about 1 pound) tart apples, pared, cored,
      and sliced
   ½ cup water
   2 tablespoons butter or margarine, melted
   ½ teaspoon salt
   1½ teaspoons cinnamon
   1 tablespoon lemon juice
   ½ cup butter or margarine
   1 cup sugar
   3 tablespoons flour
   1¼ cups crushed corn or bran flakes cold cereal*

Place apples in a 2- or 3-quart baking dish. Combine water, melted butter, salt, cinnamon, and lemon juice. Pour over apples. Cream ½ cup butter and sugar; add flour and mix well. Crush cereal. Combine with creamed mixture. Press mixture over apples. Bake, uncovered, at 375 degrees F. 30 to 35 minutes. Serve with table cream, if desired.

   CRANBERRY CRISP VARIATION: Substitute 2 or 3 cups raw cranberries for half the sliced apples. Mix the cranberries with the sliced apples and follow the same procedures as for apple crisp.

Raisin Bran is a good alternate.

Strawberry Angel Torte

   4 egg whites
   ¼ teaspoon salt
   ¼ teaspoon cream of tartar
   1 cup sugar
   1 cup heavy cream, whipped
   1 quart strawberries, washed, hulled, and halved
   1 tablespoon powdered sugar

To make torte shell, place egg whites, salt, and cream of tartar in a small bowl. Beat at high speed until eggs are frothy and begin to stiffen. Add sugar gradually and beat to very stiff peaks (8-10 minutes). Spread meringue in well-buttered 9-inch pie plate. Bake at 275 degrees F. until dry, about 1 hour.

   To make filling, spread one-half of whipped cream in the torte shell and let it stand five hours or overnight. Toss halved strawberries with powdered sugar and spoon onto torte. Top with remaining whipped cream. Serve.

   Note: Frozen strawberries may be used. Fold 1 cup (1 10-ounce package) drained strawberries into second ½ cup whipped cream and pile into meringue shells. Drizzle part or all of juice over top decoratively.

Brownie Mint Torte

   3 egg whites
   Dash of salt
   ¾ cup sugar
   ½ teaspoon vanilla
   ¾ cup fine chocolate-wafer crumbs
   1 cup whipping cream, whipped, sweetened to
      taste
   ¼ cup crushed peppermint-stick candy
   1 square unsweetened chocolate, shaved

Beat egg whites and salt until soft peaks form. Add sugar, 1 tablespoon at a time, beating after each addition until glossy. Beat in vanilla. Fold in chocolate-wafer crumbs. Spread in buttered 9-inch pie pan, piling high at sides. Bake at 325 degrees F. 35 minutes. Let cool. About 3 hours before serving, whip cream until stiff; fold in sugar to taste and the crushed peppermint candy. Pile cream mixture into chocolate shell. Chill. Before serving, trim with chocolate curls.

Apple Dumpling

  1 quart cooking apples, pared, cored, sliced
    (about 4 medium apples)
  2 tablespoons sugar
  2 tablespoons water
  1 tablespoon lemon juice

Mix ingredients well and place in an 8x8x2-inch baking pan. Cover pan with aluminum foil and bake at 350 degrees F. for 10 to 15 minutes while preparing dough (below). Remove apples from oven and cover with dough. Cut steam vents in dough. Pour sauce (recipe below) over dough. Return to oven and bake 30 minutes more, or until brown. Serve warm with hot Vanilla Sauce (below). Makes 9 servings.

Dough

  1½ cups flour
  ¼ cup sugar
  ¼ teaspoon salt
  2 teaspoons baking powder
  ½ cup vegetable shortening
  1 egg, slightly beaten
  ⅓ cup milk

Sift dry ingredients together. Cut in shortening as for pie crust, until mixture resembles coarse meal. Combine egg and milk and stir into dry ingredients. Combine thoroughly, then knead on lightly floured board about 20 times. Pat and roll out to about ½-inch thickness. Carefully place over apples. Trim excess, if necessary, so that dough fits pan.

Sauce

  ½ cup brown sugar
  ⅓ cup water
  1 tablespoon butter or margarine
  Cinnamon

Combine brown sugar, water, and butter. Boil until sugar is dissolved. Pour over dough. Sprinkle lightly with cinnamon.

Vanilla Sauce

  2 tablespoons flour
  2 tablespoons sugar
  ⅛ teaspoon salt
  ¾ cup hot water
  ¾ cup evaporated milk (one small can)
  ½ teaspoon vanilla
  2 tablespoons butter or margarine

Combine dry ingredients. Stir in hot water and bring mixture to a boil, stirring constantly. Add evaporated milk, vanilla, and butter. Reheat. Makes about 1½ cups.

Carrot Pudding

  2½ cups flour
  1¼ cups white sugar
  2½ teaspoons baking soda
  2½ teaspoons nutmeg
  ½ teaspoon cloves
  1 teaspoon salt
  2½ teaspoons cinnamon
  1¼ cups brown sugar
  2½ cups grated carrots
  2½ cups grated potatoes
  2½ cups grated apples
  2½ cups seedless raisins
  1⅓ cups dates, chopped
  1⅓ cups chopped nuts
  1¾ cups melted butter or margarine or 1⅓ cups
    suet, finely ground

Combine dry ingredients and sift together three times. Add remaining ingredients and blend well. Pour into pudding molds or cans. Two 3-pound shortening cans or one shortening can and two or three smaller cans will do. They should be well-greased, then filled no more than two-thirds full.

Cover cans with lids or use foil secured with rubber bands. Place on rack in large kettle containing about two inches of water. Steam for about two hours, or until pudding is light and dry. Makes about 3 quarts, about 25 servings.

Serve with Jiffy Lemon Sauce (page 113) or any desired pudding sauce.

Baked Custard

4 eggs, lightly beaten
2¾ cups milk
½ cup table cream
½ cup sugar
½ teaspoon salt
¾ teaspoon vanilla
Nutmeg (optional)

Beat eggs; add milk, cream, sugar, salt, and vanilla. Strain into individual custard cups set into a pan of hot water. Sprinkle nutmeg on custard, if desired. Bake at 350 degrees F. for 40 to 50 minutes. Custard is cooked when knife inserted near center comes out clean. Remove from water to cool. Chill and serve in cups. (Custard may be baked in a 1½- or 2-quart casserole instead of in individual cups.) Makes 6 to 8 servings.

Bread and Butter Pudding

6 slices white bread
2 tablespoons butter or margarine
¼ cup raisins
2 eggs
2 cups milk
¼ cup sugar
½ teaspoon nutmeg
1 teaspoon vanilla
Dash salt

Cut the crusts from the bread and butter each slice on one side. Place three slices, butter side up, in bottom of 1- to 1½-quart buttered casserole. Sprinkle with raisins. Repeat with second three slices of bread. Beat eggs slightly and add milk, sugar, nutmeg, vanilla, and salt. Pour over bread in casserole. Sprinkle top with extra nutmeg, if desired. Let stand half an hour. Bake in 350-degree F. oven for 30 minutes or until custard is firm. Serve with table cream or Quick Lemon Sauce.

Quick Lemon Sauce

1 cup powdered sugar
2 tablespoons lemon juice
Dash salt

Mix powdered sugar, lemon juice, and salt. Stir until sugar is dissolved. Add a little water if necessary to make sauce of thin consistency.

Creamy Tapioca Pudding

3 tablespoons quick-cooking tapioca
3 tablespoons sugar
⅛ teaspoon salt
2 cups milk
1 egg, separated
2 tablespoons sugar
¾ teaspoon vanilla

In a small saucepan, mix tapioca, sugar, salt, milk, and egg yolk. Let stand while preparing meringue. Beat egg white until foamy. Add 2 tablespoons sugar and beat until soft peaks form. Let stand while cooking pudding.

Cook tapioca mixture over medium heat to a full boil, stirring constantly (6 to 8 minutes). Gradually pour hot mixture into beaten egg white, stirring quickly to blend. Stir in vanilla. Cool slightly. Stir. Serve warm or chilled, garnished as desired. Makes 5 servings.

Sago Pudding

1 cup sago (old-fashioned large tapioca)
3 cups water
2 or 3 apples, peeled and sliced
⅔ cup sugar
Pinch of salt

Soak sago in water for a few minutes. Add apples, sugar, and salt. Bake at 325 degrees F. about 1 hour. Serve with hard sauce, nutmeg, and thin cream.

Hard Sauce

4 tablespoons butter or margarine
1 cup powdered sugar
1 teaspoon boiling water
Few grains salt
1 teaspoon vanilla

Cream together the butter and sugar. Add remaining ingredients and beat until smooth and fluffy. Makes about 1 cup. This sauce may be stored indefinitely in the refrigerator. If it becomes dry, add a few drops of boiling water and reheat.

Nutmeg-Pineapple Marshmallow Squares

24 large marshmallows, cut in quarters
1¾ cups milk
⅛ teaspoon salt
½ package (½ tablespoon) unflavored gelatin
¼ cup cold milk
1 cup heavy cream, whipped
½ teaspoon ground nutmeg
¼ teaspoon grated lemon rind
1 cup (8-ounce can) crushed pineapple, drained
½ cup graham cracker crumbs

Place marshmallows, milk, and salt in top of double boiler. Heat over hot water until marshmallows are melted. In the meantime, soften gelatin in ¼ cup cold milk, then stir into melted marshmallow mixture. Cool until mixture begins to thicken. Fold in whipped cream, nutmeg, lemon rind, and pineapple.

Press 4 tablespoons graham cracker crumbs in bottom of greased 9x9x2-inch pan. Gently spoon in marshmallow mixture, then top with remaining graham cracker crumbs. Chill overnight or several hours in refrigerator. Cut into squares and serve. Makes 9 servings.

Rice Pudding

2 cups cooked rice
2 cups milk
1 small can (5⅓ ounces) evaporated milk
½ cup raisins
1 tablespoon cornstarch
¼ teaspoon salt
½ cup plus 2 tablespoons sugar
2 eggs, slightly beaten
⅛ teaspoon nutmeg
⅛ teaspoon cinnamon
1 teaspoon vanilla

In a small saucepan, scald the milks together. Measure raisins into a strainer and set over boiling water just long enough to plump them. In a heavy 2- or 3-quart saucepan combine cornstarch, salt, and sugar, and blend well. Stir in hot milk mixture, stirring constantly over medium heat until thick and smooth. Add rice; reheat to a full boil. Remove from heat. Pour a little of the hot mixture into beaten eggs while stirring rapidly. Return egg mixture to hot milk and rice and stir until thickened (only a minute or two). Remove from heat. Stir in raisins, spices, and vanilla. Chill. Makes eight ½-cup servings.

Chocolate Pudding Dessert

1½ cups flour
1½ cubes (¾ cup) butter
⅔ cup chopped nuts

Combine ingredients and cut together as for pie crust, until they resemble coarse meal. Press well into a 9x13x2-inch baking pan. Bake at 325 degrees F. for 30 minutes. Remove from oven and cool.

1 cup powdered sugar
1 package (8 ounces) softened cream cheese
1 carton (9 ounces) whipped topping from freezer case   ↗

Beat together sugar and cheese until fluffy. Add one-half the whipped topping. Spread on cooled crust.

>   2 packages (3 ounces each) instant chocolate
>   pudding
>   3 cups milk

Make up pudding according to package directions, using just 3 cups milk. Spread the pudding on the cream cheese layer. Spread remaining whipped topping on pudding layer. Sprinkle with additional chopped nuts, if desired. Chill several hours or overnight. Makes 15 servings. *Note:* Butterscotch or other instant pudding flavors may also be used.

Frozen Fruit Dessert

>   1 gallon pineapple sherbet, softened
>   3 packages (10 ounces each) frozen raspberries,
>   thawed
>   5 bananas, cubed

Fold ingredients together. Put into covered plastic containers and freeze. Dessert may be made ahead of time and stored in freezer. Makes 35 servings.

FROZEN FRUIT DESSERT VARIATION: Use equal parts pineapple sherbet and vanilla ice cream, softened; frozen strawberries, thawed; and bananas cut in chunks. Combine ingredients thoroughly, being careful not to let frozen desserts melt. Refreeze.

Rhubarb Whip

>   1 pound (4 cups) rhubarb, cut in 1-inch pieces
>   ½ cup sugar
>   ¼ cup water
>   1 package (3 ounces) strawberry gelatin
>   ½ cup cold water
>   ½ cup whipping cream, whipped
>   Fresh strawberries (optional)

Combine rhubarb, sugar, and water and bring to boil. Cover and cook on low heat 8 to 10 minutes. Remove from heat. Add gelatin and stir until it dissolves (about 2 minutes). Stir in cold water. Chill until partially set. Whip until fluffy. Fold in whipped cream and pour into sherbet glasses. Chill. Garnish with fresh strawberries and additional whipped cream, if desired. Makes about eight ½-cup servings.

Pumpkin Spice Dessert

Crust

>   1 cup prepared biscuit mix
>   ½ cup quick rolled oats
>   ½ cup brown sugar
>   ¼ cup margarine

Middle Layer

>   1 can (16 ounces) pumpkin
>   1 tall can evaporated milk
>   2 eggs
>   ¾ cup sugar
>   ½ teaspoon salt
>   1 teaspoon cinnamon
>   ½ teaspoon ginger
>   ¼ teaspoon cloves

Topping

>   ½ cup pecans, chopped
>   ½ cup brown sugar
>   2 tablespoons butter
>   Whipped cream

Crust: Mix biscuit mix, rolled oats, brown sugar, and margarine until crumbly. Press into a 9x13-inch pan. Bake 10 minutes at 375 degrees F.

Middle layer: Beat pumpkin, milk, eggs, sugar, salt, and spices until well mixed. Pour over crust. Return to oven and bake 25 minutes longer.

Topping: Mix chopped pecans, brown sugar, and butter until crumbly. Sprinkle over pudding. Return to oven and bake 15 to 20 minutes longer. Cool. Serve with whipped cream. Makes 24 servings.

Nutmeg Sauce

⅔ cup sugar
1½ tablespoons cornstarch
⅛ teaspoon salt
1 cup boiling water
1 tablespoon butter
½ teaspoon nutmeg

Mix sugar, cornstarch, and salt in a small saucepan. Add boiling water and cook 3 minutes, stirring constantly. Remove from heat and add butter and nutmeg. Serve warm with steamed puddings or apple dumplings. To make a vanilla sauce, use 1 teaspoon vanilla in place of the nutmeg. If desired, add ¼ cup of rich cream.

Butterscotch Sauce

1½ cups brown sugar
⅓ cup butter or margarine
¾ cup light corn syrup
⅛ teaspoon salt
1 cup table cream (half-and-half), or evaporated milk

Cook sugar, butter, corn syrup, and salt together, stirring until sugar is completely dissolved. Add cream slowly, stirring constantly. Cook until syrup thickens, or to 228 degrees F. on a candy thermometer. Serve hot on ice cream or steamed pudding. Makes about 2 cups (10 servings).

Caramel Sauce

1½ cups sugar
1 cup hot water
1 tablespoon butter
⅛ teaspoon salt
½ teaspoon vanilla

Caramelize sugar by heating in a heavy skillet over low heat; stir constantly until sugar has melted and changed to a light brown syrup. Remove from heat and slowly stir in hot water. Return to heat and boil slowly while stirring until hard caramelized sugar completely dissolves and it reaches a temperature of 228 degrees F. on a candy thermometer (or until slightly thickened). Remove from heat and add butter, salt, and vanilla. Makes about ¾ cup, or 4 servings of 3 tablespoons each.

Autumn Sunshine Sauce

¼ cup brown sugar, firmly packed
1 egg yolk
Dash salt
1 egg white
¼ cup cream, whipped
½ teaspoon vanilla

Sift brown sugar. Add half of the sugar to egg yolk and beat until thick and light colored. Add salt to egg white and beat until foamy. Add remaining sugar 1 tablespoon at a time, beating after each addition until sugar is blended, then beat until stiff. Combine egg yolk and egg white mixtures. Fold in whipped cream and vanilla. Use as a pudding sauce.

Jiffy Lemon Sauce

½ cup sugar
2 tablespoons cornstarch
⅛ teaspoon salt
1 cup water
1 teaspoon grated lemon rind
4 tablespoons lemon juice
2 tablespoons butter

Mix sugar, cornstarch, and salt with ¼ cup water. Add remaining water and bring to a boil. Remove from heat and add remaining ingredients. Cool slightly. Makes 1¾ cups, or about 14 servings of 2 tablespoons each.

Mincemeat Pie Sauce

½ cup granulated sugar
½ cup brown sugar
2 tablespoons cornstarch
Pinch salt
1 cup water
1 tablespoon butter
½ teaspoon imitation rum flavoring

Mix sugars, cornstarch, and salt in small saucepan until well blended. Add water and bring to boil, stirring constantly. Add butter and imitation rum flavoring. Makes about 1½ cups. Serve warm with mincemeat pie.

Foamy Sauce

3 tablespoons butter or margarine
1 cup powdered sugar
2 eggs, separated
½ teaspoon vanilla
½ cup cream, whipped

Cream butter and sugar. Add egg yolk and beat over hot water. Remove from heat and fold in beaten egg whites and whipped cream. Makes about 1 cup sauce. Serve on pudding or cake.

Hot Fudge Sauce

2 squares baking chocolate
Dash of salt
1 cup sugar
1 small can (⅔ cup) evaporated milk

Combine all ingredients and cook slowly over low heat until thickened. Makes about 1 cup.

Hot Caramel Pecan Sauce

1 tablespoon flour
½ cup brown sugar
½ cup white sugar
1 tablespoon light corn syrup
¾ cup water
2 tablespoons butter
Dash of salt
Pecans

Combine all ingredients except pecans; cook as for candy. When mixture forms a soft ball in cold water, remove from heat. Add pecans. Serve on ice cream. Makes about 1 cup.

Cream Sauce for Pudding

Beat 1 egg and 1 cup powdered sugar until light. Whip 1 cup cream. When ready to serve combine the two and add ½ teaspoon vanilla.

Oatmeal Cookies with Apples and Milk

Index

Almond celery casserole, 52
Almonds with glazed broccoli, 52
Altitude adjustments, 95
Amounts of frosting to use, 95
Angel fluff, 87
Angel food cake, 86
Angel salad, 67
Appetizers:
    cheese, 7
    cheese ball, 7
    cocktail puffs, 105
    guacamole, 8
    open-face chicken sandwiches, 7
    party roll-ups, 7
    ribbon sandwiches, 7
    spinach dip, 8
    tangy shrimp, 9
Apple:
    and carrot bisque, 13
    and cherry pie, Swiss, 98
    crisp, 107
    dumpling, 107
    and lemon carrots, 51
    'n' orange pork chops, 27
    pie, 98
    salad, 64
    valley salad, 70
    and yam casserole
Applesauce fruit loaf, 78
Apricot:
    chicken, 44
    nectar, ice cream, 9
    and pineapple pie, 97
    sauce, 30
Artichoke hearts:
    Evelyn's salad, 63
    party roll-ups, 7
Autumn sunshine sauce, 113
Avocado:
    and crab salad, 68
    guacamole, 8
    stuffed, hot, 50

Baked Alaska pie, 102
Baked beans, 54
Baked chicken supreme, 37
Baked custard, 109
Baked salmon steaks, 47
Baked summer squash, 54

Banana:
    cream pie, 104
    freeze, 9
    nut bread, 76
Bar cookies:
    gingerbread, 91
    layered cookies, 94
    lemon bars, 88
Barbecued spareribs, 32
Basic cream pie, 105
Bean and bacon soup, 18
Beans. *See* Green beans
Beans, baked, 54
Bearnaise sauce, 19
Beef:
    Chateaubriand, 19
    goulash, 26
    Parmesan, 22
    party Swiss steak, 21
    and peppers, stir-fried, 22
    roast, with Yorkshire pudding, 20
    Rossini tournedos, 19
    roulade of, 25
    savory steak Italia, 22
    and seven vegetables, 24
    shepherd's pie, 27
    Stroganoff, 24
    sweet and sour, 24
    Swiss steak, 21
    Wellington, 20
Beef, ground:
    enchiladas, 26
    lasagna casserole, 29
    Lion House meat loaf, 21
    and macaroni, 29
    pasties, 28
    porcupine meatballs, 28
    Stroganoff, 24
    stuffed, 26
    sweet and sour meatballs, 28
    with zucchini, 58
Beet(s):
    Evelyn's salad, 63
    Harvard, 54
    and onions, 53
    salad, 61
Beverages:
    banana freeze, 9
    fruit freeze, 10
    fruit punch with sherbet, 10
    grenadine freeze, 9
    ice cream apricot nectar, 9
    hot tomato drink, 9
    hot zippity tomato dill drink, 8

    three-fruit slush, 10
    tomato tune-up, 9
    wassail, 10
Bienenstich cake, 83
Bisque:
    carrot and apple, 13
    crab, 16
Black bottom pie, 102
Black devil's food cake, 86
Blue cheese dressings, 73
Blueberry pie, 96
Blueberry-strawberry mold, 66
Boiled salad dressing, 72
Bordelaise sauce, 19
Boysenberry pie, 97
Bran muffins:
    quick mix, 78
    refrigerator, 79
Bread:
    applesauce, 78
    banana nut, 76
    and butter pudding, 109
    buttermilk scones, 80
    corn, 78
    cranberry, 76
    date nut, 76
    dilly casserole, 80
    orange nut, 78
    pumpkin, 81
    stuffing, 42
    whole wheat, 75
    zucchini, 80
Broccoli:
    with almonds, glazed, 52
    and chicken bake, 40
    with mustard sauce, 53
Broiled fish steaks or fillets, 46
Brown soup stock, 11
Brownie mint torte, 107
Buffet ham, 29
Butter cream filling, 83
Buttermilk dressings, 72
Buttermilk scones, 80
Butterscotch cream pie, 101
Butterscotch sauce, 113

Cabbage:
    caraway, 53
    and carrots, stewed, 53
    savory, 52
Cake recipe adjustments, 95
Cakes and cake desserts:
    angel fluff, 87
    angel food, 86

Bienenstich (sting of the bee), 82
black devil's food, 86
caramel pudding, 88
carrot, 82
cheesecake, 89
cherry cheesecake, 90
chiffon, 88
chocolate cream, 84
chocolate sheet, 84
coconut brunch, 90
German's sweet chocolate, 83
gingerbread, 91
oatmeal, 83
orange sponge, 88
peppermint angel food dessert, 87
petits fours, 89
poppy seed, 91
quick German chocolate, 84
strawberry delight, 87
whipped cream valentine, 86
whole wheat crumb, 90
Calico tossed salad, 71
California salad, 64
Canadian cheese soup, 16
Cantaloupe salad, 64
Caramel and pecan sauce, hot, 114
Caramel sauce, 113
Caraway cabbage, 53
Carrot(s):
    and apple bisque, 13
    and apples, lemon, 51
    and cabbage, stewed, 53
    cake, 82
    cookies, iced, 93
    copper penny salad, 63
    golden salad, 67
    with pineapple, 54
    pudding, 108
    salad with pineapple and coconut,
        63
    vegetable medley, 57
Cashews and chicken, 40
Casseroles:
    almond celery, 52
    chicken and broccoli bake, 40
    chicken taco pie, 42
    green bean, 58
    halibut, 46
    ham and cheese strata, 36
    ham and green noodle, 30
    lasagna, 29
    macaroni and beef bake, 29
    noodles Romanoff, 36
    potato, 54
    salmon tetrazzini, 48

shepherd's pie, 27
triple divan, 44
tuna chow mein, 49
turkey tetrazzini, 42
yam and apple, 58
zucchini, stuffed, 58, 59
zucchini with ground beef, 58
Cauliflower, company, 54
Celery and almond casserole, 52
Celery seed fruit salad dressing, 73
Chateaubriand, 19
Cheese:
    appetizers, 7
    ball, 7
    sandwich filling, 8
    sauce, 59
    and shrimp fondue, 49
    soup, Canadian, 16
Cheesecake, 89, 90
Cherry:
    and apple pie, Swiss, 98
    cheesecake, 90
    macaroons, 91
    pie, 100
Chicken:
    á la king, 43
    Alabam, 39
    apricot, 44
    bake, easy, 39
    and broccoli bake, 40
    and cashews, 40
    Cordon bleu, 41
    and corn chowder, 13
    crepes, 45
    curry salad with fruit, 70
    Hawaiian, 44
    hot stuffed avocado, 49
    Kiev, 39
    noodle soup, hearty, 15
    orange, 41
    Porter Rockwell, 40
    royale, 37
    sandwiches, open-face, 7
    in sauce, savory, 41
    stock, 11
    supreme, baked, 37
    taco pie, 42
    triple divan, 44
Chiffon cake, 87
Chili, Lion House, 18
Chilled cucumber soup, 12
Chinese spinach, 57
Chocolate:
    cake, German's sweet, 83, 84
    cream cake, 84

cream pie, 104
frostings, 84, 95
party puffs, 105
pudding dessert, 110
sheet cake, 84
Chow mein:
    casserole, tuna, 50
    pork, 35
Chowder:
    chicken and corn, 13
    clam, 16
    corn, 15
    potato and onion, 14
    Washington, 18
Cocktail puffs, 105
Coconut:
    brunch cake, 90
    cream pie, 104
    custard pie, 102
    pecan frosting, 84
    salad, with carrot and pineapple,
        63
Coleslaw, tomato, 71
Coleslaw, honey fruit, 66
Company cauliflower, 54
Cookies:
    carrot, iced, 93
    cherry macaroons, 91
    layered, 94
    oatmeal, 93
    old-fashioned filled, 94
    Scotch shortbread, 94
    spritz, 91
    sugar, 93
Copper penny salad, 63
Cordon bleu sauce, 41
Corn and chicken chowder, 13
Corn bread, 78
Corn bread stuffing, 30
Corn chowder, 15
Cornish game hens, 45
Cottage cheese fruit salad, 64
Crab:
    and avocado salad, 68
    bisque, 16
    hot stuffed avocado, 50
    seafood Newburg, 48
Cranberry:
    bread, 76
    crisp, 107
    fluff salad, 65
    pies, 97
    salads, 65, 69
Cream cheese sandwich filling, 8
Cream pie, basic, 104

Cream puffs, 105
Cream sauce for pudding, 114
Creamed onions, 55
Creamy baked halibut steaks, 46
Creamy tapioca pudding, 109
Crepes, chicken, 45
Crisp, apple or cranberry, 107
Croutons, herbed, 60
Crumb cake, whole wheat, 90
Crumb-topped baked onions, 55
Cucumber:
    sauce, 49
    set salad, 72
    soup, 13
    soup, chilled, 12
Curry, chicken salad with fruit, 69
Custard, baked, 109

Date nut bread, 76
Dessert sauces:
    apple dumpling, 108
    autumn sunshine, 113
    butterscotch, 113
    caramel, 113
    cream, for pudding, 114
    foamy, 114
    hard, 110
    hot caramel pecan, 114
    hot fudge, 114
    lemon, 109, 113
    mincemeat pie, 114
    nutmeg, 113
    pineapple, 87
    vanilla, 108
Desserts:
    apple crisp, 107
    apple dumpling, 108
    baked custard, 109
    bread and butter pudding, 109
    brownie mint torte, 107
    carrot pudding, 108
    chocolate pudding dessert, 110
    creamy tapioca pudding, 109
    frozen fruit, 112
    nutmeg-pineapple-marshmallow
        squares, 110
    pumpkin spice dessert, 112
    rhubarb whip, 112
    rice pudding, 110
    sago pudding, 109
    strawberry angel torte, 107
    See also Cakes; Cookies; Pies
Devil's food cake, 86
Dill—sour cream sauce, 48
Dilly casserole bread, 80

Dinner rolls, 75
Dips:
    guacamole, 8
    spinach, 8
Divan, triple, 44
Dreamy fruit salad, 70
Dressings. See Salad Dressings

Easy cherry cheesecake, 90
Easy chicken bake, 39
Easy lasagna casserole, 29
Easy petits fours, 89
Eclairs, 105
Egg salad sandwich filling, 8
Enchiladas, beef, 26
Evelyn's salad, 63

Famous fruit salad dressing, 74
Filling, butter cream, 83
Filling, raisin, 94
Fillings, sandwich, 8
Fish:
    halibut au gratin, 47
    halibut steaks, creamy baked, 46
    lemon, baked, 46
    salmon mousse, 48
    salmon roll, 47
    salmon steaks, baked, 47
    salmon tetrazzini, 48
    seafood Newburg, 49
    steaks or fillets, broiled, 46
    tuna chow mein casserole, 50
Foamy sauce, 114
Four-bean salad, 61
Four-step black bottom pie, 102
Freeze:
    banana, 9
    fruit, 10
    grenadine, 9
French dressing, Lion House, 74
French fruit dressing, 64
Fresh fruit mold, 67
Fresh strawberry pie, 100
Frosting:
    amounts to use, 94
    for carrot cake, 82
    chocolate, 84, 95
    for chocolate sheet cake, 84
    coconut pecan, 83
    for oatmeal cake, 83
    orange, 93
    orange butter glaze, 94
    for petits fours, 89
Frozen blue cheese dressing, 73
Frozen fruit dessert, 112

Frozen fruit salad, 64
Fruit:
    angel salad, 67
    banana freeze, 9
    and cottage cheese salad, 64
    dessert, frozen, 112
    dressing, French, 64
    freeze, 10
    fresh fruit mold, 67
    grenadine freeze, 9
    loaf, applesauce, 78
    mold, fresh, 67
    muffins, Lion House, 81
    princess salad, 66
    punch with sherbet, 10
    salad, 65
    salad, dreamy, 70
    salad, frozen, 64
    salad, orange cream, 70
    salad, six-cup, 66
    salad dressing, celery seed, 73
    salad dressing, famous, 74
    sauce for ham, 29
    slaw, 66
    slaw, honey, 66
    three-fruit slush, 10
    See also Cakes and Cake Desserts;
        Pies; Desserts
Fudge sauce, hot, 114

Game hens, 45
Gazpacho, 13
German green beans, 51
German chocolate cake, quick, 84
German's sweet chocolate cake, 83
Gingerbread, 91
Glaze:
    maple syrup and cider, for ham, 28
    orange, for ham, 27
    orange butter, 94
Glazed broccoli with almonds, 52
Golden carrot salad, 67
Golden squash soup, 14
Gooseberry pie, 97
Goulash, beef, 26
Grapefruit salad, 65
Grapefruit with lime gelatin and
    shrimp, 68
Grasshopper pie, 106
Gravy thickener (roux), 12
Greek tossed salad (salata), 61
Green bean(s):
    casserole, 58
    four-bean salad, 63
    German, 51

Hungarian, 56
Italian, 53
Parisienne, 51
Parmesan, 56
sesame, 52
south of the border, 51
Green goddess salad, 60
Green noodles and ham casserole, 30
Green salad, 61
Green sauce, 36
Guacamole, 8

Halibut au gratin, 46
Halibut steaks, creamy baked, 46
Ham:
    buffet, 29
    and cheese strata, 36
    and green noodle casserole, 30
    loaf, 35
    with maple sugar and cider glaze,
        28
    quiche Lorraine, 42
    roll-ups, party, 30
    sandwich filling, 8
    triple divan, 44
Hard sauce, 110
Harvard beets, 54
Hawaiian chicken, 44
Hearty chicken noodle soup, 15
Herbed croutons, 60
High-altitude recipe adjustments, 95
Honey butter, 75
Honey fruit slaw, 66
Honeyed onions, 56
Hot caramel pecan sauce, 114
Hot fudge sauce, 114
Hot stuffed avocado, 50
Hot tomato drink, 9
Hot zippity tomato dill drink, 8
Hungarian green beans, 56

Ice cream apricot nectar, 9
Iced carrot cookies, 93
Icings. See Frostings

Jiffy lemon sauce, 113

Key lime pie, 106

Lamb: shepherd's pie, 27
Lamb stew, 20
Lasagna casserole, 29
Layered cookies, 94
Lemon:
    bars, 88

carrots and apples, 51
cream pie, 100
fish bake, 46
meringue pie, 100
sauce (dessert), 109, 113
sauce for vegetables, 59
Lemonade chiffon pie, 100
Lime:
    gelatin, shrimp, and grapefruit
        salad, 68
    and pear salad or dessert, 70
    pie, key, 106
Lion House:
    chicken crepes, 45
    chili, 18
    French dressing, 74
    fruit muffins, 81
    meat loaf, 21
    pie dough, 96
    taffy, 4
Lobster: seafood Newburg, 49

Macaroni and beef bake, 29
Macaroni and tomato soup, 15
Macaroons, cherry, 91
Mandarin salad, 67
Maple syrup and cider glaze, for
    ham, 28
Meat loaf, Lion House, 21
Meatballs, porcupine, 28
Meatballs, sweet and sour, 24
Meats. See Beef; Beef, ground;
    Ham; Lamb; Pork
Mexican taco salad, 71
Mincemeat pie sauce, 114
Minestrone, 12
Mint sauce for lamb, 35
Mock hollandaise sauce, 59
Mongolian hot pot soup, 11
Mousse, salmon, 48
Muffins:
    fruit, Lion House, 81
    quick bran mix, 78
    refrigerator bran, 79
Mustard:
    cream dressing, 73
    ring, 36
    sauce for ham, 27
    sauce for ham loaf, 35

Noodles Romanoff, 36
Nutmeg sauce, 113
Nutmeg-pineapple-marshmallow
    squares, 110

Oatmeal cake, 83
Oatmeal cookies, 93
Onions(s):
    baked, crumb-topped, 55
    and beets, 53
    creamed, 55
    honeyed, 56
    and potato chowder, 14
Open-face chicken sandwiches, 7
Orange:
    'n' apple pork chops, 27
    butter glaze, 94
    chicken, 41
    cream fruit salad, 70
    nut bread, 78
    rolls, 79
    sponge cake, 88
Oriental rice, 36

Parmesan beef, 22
Party ham roll-ups, 30
Party roll-ups, 7
Party Swiss steak, 20
Pasties, beef, 28
Pastry, for pies, 96
Pear(s):
    blush salad, 66
    and lime salad or dessert, 70
    princess salad, 66
Peppermint angel food dessert, 87
Peppers and stir-fried beef, 22
Petits fours, 89
Pie dough, Lion House, 96
Pie sauce, mincemeat, 114
Pies:
    apple, 98
    apricot-pineapple, 97
    baked Alaska, 102
    basic cream, 104
    blueberry, 96
    boysenberry or gooseberry, 97
    butterscotch cream, 101
    cherry, 100
    coconut custard, 102
    cranberry, 97
    four-step black bottom, 102
    fresh strawberry, 100
    grasshopper, 106
    key lime, 106
    lemonade chiffon, 100
    lemon cream, 16
    lemon meringue, 100
    pralines and cream, 106
    pumpkin, 105
    pumpkin chiffon, 104